Criminal Psychology

Explore the Nature of the Criminal Mind and Discover the Secrets of Profiling and Lie Detection

Morris Hunt

Table of Contents

Chapter One: Introduction and Origins

Criminal psychology, an essential subfield of forensic psychology, is often misunderstood and misrepresented. Its scope extends far beyond the dramatic portrayals seen in popular media. At its core, criminal psychology involves the study of the thoughts, intentions, actions, and reactions of criminals and all that partakes in the criminal or justice system.

The breadth of criminal psychology is vast, encompassing a range of activities that include but are not limited to the psychological assessment of criminals, understanding the psychological impact of crime on victims, assisting in criminal investigations, and providing expert testimony in legal proceedings. Moreover, criminal psychologists often engage in the development and evaluation of treatment programs for offenders, aiming to reduce recidivism and facilitate rehabilitation.

Psychological Assessment of Offenders

A crucial aspect of criminal psychology involves the psychological assessment of individuals who have committed crimes. These assessments serve multiple purposes: they can help determine a suspect's competency to stand trial, provide insights into their mental state at the time of the offense, and assist in forming a basis for sentencing recommendations. This process often involves a comprehensive examination, including clinical interviews, psychometric testing, and review of criminal and personal history.

Role in Criminal Investigations

Criminal psychologists also play a vital role in criminal investigations. Through offender profiling, they assist law enforcement agencies in narrowing down potential suspects and understanding the behavior patterns of serial offenders. This process involves analyzing crime scenes, understanding the nature of the offense, and drawing psychological inferences about the perpetrator.

Expert Testimony and Legal Consultation

In the courtroom, criminal psychologists provide expert testimony, particularly in cases where the mental state of the defendant is a pivotal issue. Their expertise can help juries and judges understand complex psychological issues related to criminal behavior, such as the impact of mental disorders on culpability. Additionally, they offer insights into witness credibility, jury decision-making, and the psychological aspects of victim testimony.

Treatment and Rehabilitation of Offenders

Beyond assessment and investigation, criminal psychologists are deeply involved in the treatment and rehabilitation of offenders. This includes designing and implementing intervention programs aimed at reducing criminal behavior and preparing inmates for successful reintegration into society. These programs are tailored to address various factors, including substance abuse, violent behavior, and sexual offenses, and are grounded in psychological principles and research.

Understanding the Impact on Victims

Criminal psychology also addresses the impact of crime on victims. This involves studying the psychological effects of being a victim of a crime and providing support and counseling to help them cope with the aftermath. The field also explores the dynamics of victim-offender interactions and the factors that influence how individuals become victims.

Relevance in Criminology

Criminal psychology provides a crucial link between psychological theory and criminal behavior, offering insights that can help prevent crime and improve the effectiveness of the criminal justice system. By understanding the psychological factors that contribute to criminal behavior, criminologists can develop more effective strategies for crime prevention and intervention.

Historical Evolution

The origins of criminal psychology can be traced back to the late 19th and early 20th centuries. During this period, pioneers in psychology and psychiatry began to explore the links between mental illness and criminal behavior. One of the earliest figures in this field was Cesare Lombroso, an Italian criminologist and physician who, in the late 1800s, proposed that criminality was inherited and that criminals could be identified by physical defects. This theory, now largely discredited, marked one of the first attempts to scientifically study criminals.

In the early 20th century, as psychology established itself as a scientific discipline, more nuanced approaches to studying criminal behavior emerged. Psychologists like Sigmund Freud and his followers began to explore the psychological motivations behind criminal acts, focusing on unconscious drives and childhood experiences. While some of Freud's ideas have been critiqued or refined, his influence in bringing psychological perspectives to the study of criminal behavior is undeniable.

The mid-20th century witnessed a shift towards behavioral and sociological approaches to criminal psychology. Behaviorists like B.F. Skinner emphasized the role of environmental factors and learning in shaping behavior, including criminality. This period also saw the rise of sociological theories, such as strain theory and social learning theory, which posited that criminal behavior was a result of societal structures and peer influences, rather than innate tendencies or psychological pathology alone.

Forensic psychology, a related but distinct field, began to take shape in the 20th century. This field applied psychological principles to legal issues, including assessments of competency to stand trial, insanity defenses, and the reliability of eyewitness testimony. The development of forensic psychology played a crucial role in integrating psychological insights into the criminal justice system.

The latter part of the 20th century saw the emergence of criminal profiling as a significant tool in law enforcement. Profilers began to use psychological principles to predict the characteristics of unknown offenders based on crime scene evidence. This period also marked a growing interest in victimology - the study of victims of crime - and how their interactions with offenders and the criminal justice system impact their psychological well-being.

The 21st century has introduced new dimensions to criminal psychology, with advancements in technology and neuroscience. Neuroscientific research has begun to uncover the brain mechanisms underlying criminal behavior, while digital technologies have led to the rise of cyberpsychology – the study of the psychological aspects of cybercrime. These developments have significantly expanded the tools and methods available to criminal psychologists.

Today, criminal psychology is a diverse field that integrates insights from psychology, criminology, sociology, neuroscience, and law. It employs a range of methods, from empirical research to clinical assessments, to understand, prevent, and respond to criminal behavior. This evolution reflects an ongoing effort to comprehensively understand the complex interplay of factors that contribute to criminality.

Key Theories and Models

Criminal psychology, as a field, rests on a bedrock of diverse theories and models that seek to explain the complex nature of criminal behavior. These theories, developed over decades, offer varying perspectives and insights, each contributing to a more nuanced understanding of what drives individuals to commit crimes.

Classical Criminology

Classical criminology emerged in the 18th century as a reaction to the arbitrary and often brutal legal systems of the time. Key figures like Cesare Beccaria and Jeremy Bentham spearheaded this movement. Beccaria, in his seminal work "On Crimes and Punishments" (1764), criticized the inhumane treatment of criminals and the inefficiency of the criminal justice system.

The core idea of classical criminology is the notion of free will. It posits that individuals are rational beings who possess the ability to make choices. In this context, criminal behavior is seen as a result of rational calculation. Individuals weigh the benefits and consequences of their actions — if the perceived pleasures of the crime outweigh the pains of potential punishment, they may choose to commit the crime.

This theory had profound implications for the legal system. Classical criminologists advocated for a more systematic and just approach to punishment. They argued for the need for laws to be clear, public, and applied uniformly, insisting that punishments should be proportionate to the crime and serve as a deterrent. This led to significant reforms, emphasizing rationality and fairness in legal proceedings and punishments.

Positivist Criminology

In the 19th century, a shift occurred with the advent of positivist criminology. This approach was largely influenced by the scientific discoveries of the time, particularly in biology and psychology. Cesare Lombroso, often regarded as the father of modern criminology, is a prominent figure in this school. His work marked a significant departure from classical thinking.

Positivist criminology posits that criminal behavior is not a result of free will but is determined by factors outside the individual's control. Lombroso's theory of the 'born criminal' suggested that criminality was inherited and could be identified through physical characteristics (a concept known as atavism). This marked a move towards understanding criminal behavior through empirical and scientific methods, focusing on biological, psychological, and sociological factors.

While Lombroso's theories on atavism have been largely discredited, his emphasis on scientific analysis in understanding criminal behavior laid the groundwork for modern criminological studies. This approach led to the development of various branches in criminology, including biological, psychological, and sociological theories of crime.

Positivist criminology has evolved to include a wide range of theories that explore the complexities of human behavior. Modern criminology often integrates elements of both classical and positivist schools, recognizing the role of individual choice while also considering the various external factors that influence criminal behavior.

Psychoanalytic Theory

Sigmund Freud's psychoanalytic theory, while initially developed to understand human personality and psychological disorders, has significantly influenced the field of criminal psychology. Freud's model of the psyche, comprising the id, ego, and superego, forms the basis of this theory.

- The **id** represents primal urges and desires. When these urges are repressed or unfulfilled, they can manifest in antisocial ways.

- The **ego**, which mediates between the id and the external world, can become overwhelmed or ineffective in managing these urges.

- The **superego**, embodying moral standards and conscience, when underdeveloped or in conflict with the id, might lead to criminal acts as expressions of guilt or as means of seeking punishment.

Freud suggested that unresolved internal conflicts, often rooted in childhood experiences, play a crucial role in shaping adult behavior. Traumatic events or dysfunctional family dynamics can lead to the development of defense mechanisms, which may manifest as criminal behavior in an attempt to resolve these unconscious conflicts.

This perspective offers a framework for understanding criminal behavior as a symptom of deeper psychological issues. It implies that addressing the root causes of these internal conflicts, through methods like psychoanalysis, could be pivotal in rehabilitating criminals.

Behavioral Theory

Behavioral theory, notably advanced by B.F. Skinner, diverges significantly from psychoanalytic theory by focusing on observable behavior rather than internal mental states. This theory posits that all behavior, including criminal behavior, is learned through interaction with the environment.

Skinner's concept of operant conditioning is central to behavioral theory. It suggests that behaviors are shaped by their consequences – rewards increase the likelihood of a behavior, while punishments decrease it. In the context of criminal behavior, this implies that if criminal acts are rewarded or not sufficiently punished, they are more likely to be repeated.

The environment plays a crucial role in shaping behavior. This includes family dynamics, peer influence, and societal norms. For instance, a child who observes and receives reinforcement for aggressive behavior is more likely to develop antisocial tendencies.

Albert Bandura's social learning theory, an extension of behavioral theory, emphasizes the role of modeling in learning behavior. Individuals can learn criminal behavior by observing and imitating others, especially if those behaviors appear to be rewarded.

Behavioral theory suggests that changing environmental factors and reinforcement patterns can alter criminal behavior. This has led to the development of behavioral modification programs and policies aimed at altering the consequences of criminal actions to deter crime.

Social Learning Theory

Albert Bandura's social learning theory, developed in the 1960s and 70s, revolutionized the understanding of how behavior is acquired and maintained. This theory asserts that much of human learning, including the development of criminal behavior, occurs in a social context.

- **Observational Learning:** Individuals learn behaviors by observing others, particularly those they consider role models. This includes parents, peers, or even media figures. If a child observes a significant figure engaging in criminal behavior and being rewarded for it (e.g., gaining money, respect, or power), they may imitate this behavior.

- **Reinforcement and Punishment:** The likelihood of a behavior being repeated is influenced by the consequences it receives. Reinforcement (positive or negative) encourages a behavior, while punishment discourages it. In the context of crime, if the perceived rewards of crime outweigh the consequences, an individual is more likely to engage in criminal behavior.

- **Vicarious Reinforcement:** People not only learn from the consequences of their own actions but also from the consequences experienced by others. Seeing others successfully engage in crime without negative repercussions can be a powerful motivator.

Social learning theory has significant implications for understanding and addressing criminal behavior. It suggests that interventions should focus not only on the individual but also on their social environment. This includes programs aimed at providing positive role models, altering peer group dynamics, and controlling the depiction of crime in media.

Strain Theory

Robert K. Merton's strain theory, introduced in the 1930s, is a significant sociological theory that examines the societal structures that influence behavior. Merton argued that society's structure creates pressure on individuals to achieve certain culturally defined goals, often emphasizing material success.

The central premise of strain theory is the disjunction between societal goals and the legitimate means available to achieve them. Merton proposed that when individuals are unable to achieve societal goals (e.g., wealth, status) through socially approved methods (due to factors like poverty, educational inequality), they experience strain or frustration, leading some to engage in criminal behavior as an alternative way to achieve these goals.

Merton outlined several ways individuals adapt to this strain:

- **Conformity:** Pursuing cultural goals through legitimate means.

- **Innovation:** Using illegitimate means to achieve cultural goals (often associated with criminal behavior).

- **Ritualism:** Abandoning cultural goals but continuing to adhere to legitimate means.

- **Retreatism:** Rejecting both cultural goals and legitimate means (associated with withdrawal from society).

- **Rebellion:** Rejecting and attempting to change both the cultural goals and the means.

Strain theory has significant implications for understanding the socio-economic roots of crime. It suggests that policies aimed at reducing criminal behavior should focus on reducing the disparities in access to legitimate means of achieving societal goals, such as improving education and employment opportunities.

Control Theory

Control theory, particularly as developed by Travis Hirschi in the late 1960s, offers a unique perspective in criminology by asking why people refrain from criminal behavior, rather than why they engage in it. Hirschi's "Social Bond Theory" is central to this approach.

- **Attachment:** The emotional and psychological bonds an individual has with others, particularly significant figures like parents, teachers, and peers. Strong attachments encourage individuals to conform to the expectations of these figures.

- **Commitment:** The investment an individual has in conventional activities and goals, such as education and career. The greater the investment, the more an individual has to lose by engaging in criminal behavior.

- **Involvement:** Participation in conventional activities, like sports, clubs, or community services, occupies an individual's time and energy, reducing the opportunity and inclination for deviance.

- **Belief:** Acceptance of social norms and values. When individuals believe strongly in societal rules, they are less likely to violate them.

Control theory has significant implications for crime prevention strategies. It suggests that strengthening community and familial ties, increasing educational and occupational opportunities, and fostering involvement in community activities can reduce criminal behavior. Programs aimed at enhancing these social bonds, especially in youth, are often based on the principles of this theory.

Labeling Theory

Labeling theory, emerging in the mid-20th century and associated with sociologists like Howard Becker, focuses on the societal reaction to deviance and its consequences. This theory is a significant part of the symbolic interactionist perspective in sociology.

- **Primary Deviance:** Initial acts of deviance that may or may not result in the individual being labeled as deviant.

- **Secondary Deviance:** Behavior that results from the societal reaction to the label of deviance. Once labeled, individuals may accept this label as part of their identity and act accordingly.

- **Self-Fulfilling Prophecy:** The concept that labeling can create a self-fulfilling prophecy where the individual internalizes the label, leading to further deviance. This can exacerbate a cycle of criminal behavior.

Labeling theory highlights the role of societal reactions and the stigma associated with being labeled a criminal. The process of labeling can marginalize individuals, limiting their opportunities for rehabilitation and reintegration into society.

This theory has profound implications for criminal justice policies, advocating for approaches that avoid stigmatizing labels. It supports rehabilitative rather than punitive measures and emphasizes the importance of societal support in the reintegration of offenders.

The Way of a Criminal Psychologist

At the heart of a criminal psychologist's role is offender profiling and investigative support. This function involves an in-depth analysis of criminal behavior to assist law enforcement agencies. Profilers scrutinize crime scenes, study patterns of behavior, and apply psychological principles to infer characteristics of the unknown offender. Their expertise is not just limited to profiling; they also contribute significantly to the broader aspects of criminal investigations, offering insights into criminal motives and predicting future actions.

Assessment and evaluation form another critical component of their responsibilities. Criminal psychologists conduct comprehensive evaluations of individuals within the criminal justice system, often for purposes such as determining competency to stand trial or assessing the risk of reoffending. These evaluations, conducted through clinical interviews, psychological testing, and review of personal history, inform crucial legal decisions and have significant implications for the outcomes of cases.

The treatment and rehabilitation of offenders is an area where criminal psychologists contribute profoundly. They develop and implement treatment programs that address underlying psychological issues such as aggression, substance abuse, and mental health disorders. These programs, often based on therapeutic models like cognitive-behavioral therapy, aim to reduce recidivism and facilitate the successful reintegration of offenders into society.

An often understated yet vital aspect of their role is engaging in research and development. Criminal psychologists actively participate in research to enhance the understanding of criminal behavior and the effectiveness of various interventions. This research covers a broad spectrum, from the psychological underpinnings of criminality to the efficacy of rehabilitation programs, and is essential for the evolution of evidence-based practices in the field.

In the legal arena, criminal psychologists often emerge as key figures by providing expert testimony in court cases. They present findings from psychological evaluations, offer opinions on mental health issues, and elucidate complex psychological concepts for the jury and judge. Their expertise, particularly in cases where mental state or competency is in question, can be pivotal in influencing legal outcomes.

Beyond working with offenders, criminal psychologists also focus on supporting victims of crime. They provide counseling services to help victims cope with the psychological aftermath of criminal acts and advocate for victims' rights. Understanding the impact of crime on victims is crucial for a holistic approach to criminal justice.

Furthermore, criminal psychologists have a significant role in policy development and advisory roles. They offer expert advice to policymakers, law enforcement agencies, and correctional institutions, guiding the development of policies and practices grounded in psychological knowledge. This contribution is crucial in shaping public policy related to criminal justice and mental health.

Lastly, their role encompasses education and training. Criminal psychologists are involved in teaching, conducting workshops, and developing training programs for law enforcement personnel, legal professionals, and fellow psychologists. This educational aspect ensures that the insights gained from the field of criminal psychology are disseminated and applied effectively across various sectors of the criminal justice system.

The Ethical Dilemmas

The role of a criminal psychologist often entails making difficult decisions that have far-reaching consequences, not just for the individuals directly involved but also for the broader aspects of justice and societal wellbeing.

Central to these ethical considerations is the dilemma of dual relationships. Criminal psychologists frequently find themselves in a position where their professional responsibilities to the legal system might conflict with their duty to the individuals they assess or treat. For instance, when conducting evaluations for legal purposes, their findings can significantly impact an individual's legal fate. This dual responsibility – to their client or patient and to the legal system – can create conflicts of interest, challenging the psychologist to balance these competing demands while upholding professional ethics.

Confidentiality, a cornerstone of psychological practice, presents another area of ethical complexity in criminal psychology. The general expectation of client-therapist confidentiality becomes nuanced when dealing with criminal cases. There are circumstances, such as when an individual poses a risk to themselves or others, where breaking confidentiality becomes not just a legal obligation but a moral imperative. Determining when to breach this confidentiality requires careful ethical consideration and often, a deep understanding of both legal mandates and psychological ethics.

Informed consent is a critical ethical principle in any psychological practice. However, in the context of criminal psychology, obtaining truly informed consent poses unique challenges. Individuals undergoing psychological evaluation often do so under legal compulsion. This raises questions about the voluntariness of their consent and the extent to which they understand the implications of the assessment, particularly how it might be used in legal proceedings.

The use of psychological techniques and knowledge in criminal psychology also brings forth ethical dilemmas. Techniques such as criminal profiling and risk assessment, while valuable, can sometimes lead to overgeneralizations or biases, potentially impacting the fairness of legal proceedings. Ensuring these techniques are used responsibly and accurately is a persistent ethical challenge, requiring ongoing reflection and adherence to evidence-based practices.

The treatment of offenders is another area fraught with ethical considerations. Psychologists must navigate the fine line between respecting the rights and autonomy of the offender and ensuring public safety. This is particularly challenging when dealing with offenders who have committed heinous crimes and yet, as patients, are entitled to compassionate and effective treatment.

Further complicating the ethical landscape is the role of criminal psychologists as expert witnesses in legal proceedings. Their testimony can significantly influence the outcome of trials. The ethical imperative here is to ensure that their testimony is not only based on sound psychological knowledge but is also presented in a way that is understandable and does not unduly sway judicial proceedings. Balancing the duty to provide expert insight with the need to avoid becoming an advocate for one side or the other is a delicate task.

Moreover, working in the field of criminal psychology often involves exposure to disturbing cases and sensitive information. Maintaining professional detachment while providing empathetic care is essential to avoid burnout and secondary trauma. Psychologists must be mindful of their own mental health and ethical boundaries to continue providing effective and ethical care.

Chapter Two: The Criminal Mind

Understanding the psychological traits common among criminals is a complex and nuanced aspect of criminal psychology. While not all individuals exhibiting these traits engage in criminal behavior, research indicates that certain personality characteristics are more prevalent in criminal populations.

- **Antisocial Personality Traits**: One of the most significant traits linked to criminal behavior is antisocial personality characteristics, often formalized as Antisocial Personality Disorder (ASPD). Individuals with ASPD tend to exhibit a lack of regard for the moral or legal standards in the local culture. This manifests as a failure to conform to social norms, deceitfulness, impulsivity, irritability, aggression, recklessness, and a lack of remorse.

- **Aggression and Violence**: Aggression, whether physical or verbal, is a trait commonly observed in individuals who engage in criminal acts. This includes a propensity for violent behavior, which can be reactive (in response to perceived threats or provocations) or proactive (used as a means to an end). It's important to note that aggression alone does not necessarily lead to criminal behavior, but when combined with other factors, it can be a significant risk factor.

- **Impulsivity**: Impulsivity, or the tendency to act without forethought or consideration of consequences, is a prominent characteristic in many criminal profiles. It contributes to poor decision-making and a propensity for risky behavior, often leading to situations where criminal activity becomes more likely.

- **Narcissism**: Some criminals exhibit narcissistic traits, including a grandiose sense of self-importance, a need for admiration, and a lack of empathy for others. Narcissism in criminals can manifest in manipulative or exploitative behaviors and a belief that one is above the law.

- **Machiavellianism**: This trait refers to a person's tendency to be manipulative and deceitful for personal gain. Individuals high in Machiavellianism often use cunning and duplicity in their interactions with others and may engage in criminal activities if they believe it will help them achieve their goals.

- **Borderline Personality Traits**: In some cases, traits associated with Borderline Personality Disorder, such as unstable relationships, intense emotions, and impulsive behaviors, can be linked to criminal activities. These individuals may engage in criminal acts during intense emotional states or as a result of impulsive decision-making.

- **Lack of Empathy and Remorse**: A diminished capacity for empathy and remorse is a common trait among criminals, particularly those who commit severe offenses. This lack of emotional connection to others makes it easier for them to engage in harmful behaviors without the inhibitory effects of guilt or compassion.

- **Risk-Seeking Behavior**: A propensity for seeking out risky or thrilling experiences can be another trait common among individuals who engage in criminal activities. This desire for excitement can lead to engagement in illegal activities that are perceived as exhilarating or daring.

- **Poor Behavioral Controls**: This includes a tendency to react adversely to minor irritations or frustrations, often leading to disproportionate and sometimes violent responses. Poor behavioral control is a significant risk factor for criminal behavior, particularly in situations that escalate quickly.

Neurobiological Factors

The exploration of neurobiological factors in criminal behavior marks a significant advancement in criminal psychology, shedding light on how certain brain structures and functions may influence criminal tendencies. This field of study intertwines neurobiology with psychology to unravel the complexities of the criminal mind.

The human brain is an intricate organ, and its functioning is pivotal in determining behavior. In the context of criminal behavior, neurobiological research has focused on specific areas of the brain and neurotransmitter systems to understand their role in predisposing individuals to criminal acts.

The Prefrontal Cortex

The prefrontal cortex, located at the front of the brain, is crucial for decision-making, impulse control, and moderating social behavior. Research has shown that dysfunction in this area can lead to impulsivity, poor judgment, and a propensity for aggressive behavior – traits often observed in criminal offenders. Studies using neuroimaging techniques like fMRI (Functional Magnetic Resonance Imaging) have revealed that individuals with a history of violent criminal behavior often exhibit reduced activity or abnormalities in the prefrontal cortex.

The Amygdala

The amygdala, a small, almond-shaped structure deep within the brain, plays a critical role in processing emotions, especially fear and aggression. Abnormalities in the amygdala have been linked to aggression and violence, which are common in certain types of criminal behavior. For instance, individuals with a reduced amygdala response to threatening stimuli might have a diminished fear response, potentially leading to riskier and more aggressive behaviors without the normal inhibitory effects of fear.

Neurotransmitter Systems

Neurotransmitters, the brain's chemical messengers, also play a significant role in criminal behavior. For example, serotonin, a neurotransmitter associated with mood regulation, has been linked to aggression and impulse control. Low levels of serotonin have been found in individuals with a history of violent behavior, suggesting a neurochemical predisposition to such acts.

Dopamine, another neurotransmitter, is associated with reward and pleasure systems in the brain. Dysregulation in dopamine pathways has been implicated in addiction, risk-taking behaviors, and certain personality disorders, all of which can be relevant in the context of criminal behavior.

Genetics and Environmental Interactions

While examining the role of brain structures and functions, it's essential to consider genetic factors. Genetic predispositions can influence the development and functioning of the brain. However, the expression of these genetic factors is often modulated by environmental influences. For instance, childhood trauma, abuse, or prolonged exposure to stress can alter brain chemistry and structure, potentially leading to behavioral patterns associated with criminality.

Neurodevelopmental Factors

Neurodevelopmental factors during prenatal and early life stages can significantly impact brain development. Factors such as prenatal exposure to toxins, maternal drug use, malnutrition, and early childhood trauma can lead to atypical brain development, which may predispose individuals to criminal behavior later in life.

Legal and Ethical Implications

The findings from neurobiological research have profound implications for the criminal justice system. They raise questions about culpability, free will, and the extent to which biological factors can be held responsible for criminal behavior. This has led to debates about sentencing, rehabilitation, and the possibility of using neurobiological evidence in court proceedings.

Environmental Influences

The impact of upbringing and social environment on the development of criminal tendencies has been a subject of extensive study and debate.

Family and Upbringing

The family environment plays a pivotal role in an individual's early development and can significantly influence their later behavior. Various aspects of family life, including parenting styles, family structure, and the presence of abuse or neglect, have been linked to criminal behavior.

- **Parenting Styles**: Research suggests that certain parenting styles, particularly those that are neglectful or excessively harsh, can lead to the development of antisocial behavior in children. In contrast, supportive and attentive parenting has been associated with lower risks of such behavior.

- **Family Structure**: The structure of a family, including factors such as single parenthood, the presence of step-parents, or large family size, can also impact the likelihood of criminal behavior. However, it's important to note that these factors do not directly cause criminality but may contribute to conditions that increase risk.

- **Abuse and Neglect**: Exposure to abuse (physical, emotional, or sexual) and neglect during childhood is a significant risk factor for the development of criminal behavior. Such experiences can lead to a range of psychological issues, including aggression, impulse control problems, and a propensity for violence.

Socioeconomic Status and Neighborhood Environment

Socioeconomic status (SES) and the characteristics of one's neighborhood environment are also critical in understanding the development of criminal behavior.

- **Poverty and Economic Strain**: Living in poverty or experiencing economic strain can increase the risk of engaging in criminal activities. Economic hardship may lead to involvement in crimes such as theft, drug dealing, or other illegal activities as a means of financial survival.

- **Neighborhood Influences**: Growing up in a neighborhood characterized by high crime rates, gang presence, or a lack of social cohesion can normalize criminal behavior and provide opportunities for engaging in illegal activities. The neighborhood environment can also impact access to positive role models and resources for healthy development.

Education and Peer Influences

Education and peer relationships are significant environmental factors that can influence the likelihood of criminal behavior.

- **Educational Experiences**: Negative experiences in school, such as academic failure, truancy, or expulsion, are linked to higher risks of criminal behavior. Education provides not only academic skills but also socialization and opportunities for positive development, which can be protective against criminal behavior.

- **Peer Influences**: Peers can have a profound impact on behavior, particularly during adolescence. Association with delinquent peers is a strong predictor of criminal behavior. Peer groups can influence norms, values, and behaviors, sometimes encouraging or facilitating criminal activities.

Cultural and Societal Factors

The broader cultural and societal context also plays a role in shaping individual behavior.

- **Cultural Norms and Values**: Cultural norms and values can influence attitudes towards criminal behavior. In some contexts, certain criminal activities may be normalized or even valorized, increasing their likelihood.

- **Media Influence**: Exposure to violence or criminal behavior in the media can also impact attitudes and behaviors. While media exposure alone is not a direct cause of criminal behavior, it can contribute to the normalization of violence and aggression.

Cognitive Distortions in Criminals

Cognitive distortions are essentially thought patterns that deviate from rational and logical thinking. They are biased perspectives that individuals develop based on their experiences and internal beliefs. In the realm of criminal behavior, these distorted cognitions can lead to misconceptions about oneself, others, and society, influencing the individual's actions and decisions.

Types of Cognitive Distortions

- **Justification and Rationalization**: One of the most common cognitive distortions in criminal behavior is the tendency to justify or rationalize one's actions. Criminals often construct a narrative in their minds that makes their behavior seem acceptable or necessary, even if it is harmful or illegal. This rationalization can take the form of blaming others, externalizing responsibility, or minimizing the seriousness of the offense.

- **Sense of Entitlement**: Some criminals exhibit a distorted sense of entitlement, believing they have the right to break the law or harm others to get what they want. This distortion leads to a lack of empathy and disregard for the rights and feelings of others.

- **Victim Stance**: Another common distortion is perceiving oneself as the victim, even when one is the perpetrator. This mindset involves feeling that the world is unjust and that one's criminal actions are a response to being wronged or oppressed by others or society at large.

- **Black-and-White Thinking**: Also known as 'all-or-nothing' thinking, this distortion involves seeing the world in extremes, without any middle ground. For criminals, this can mean categorizing people as entirely good or bad, or viewing situations in terms of absolute success or failure, leading to rigid and often unrealistic perceptions.

- **Overgeneralization**: This occurs when individuals draw broad conclusions based on a single event or piece of evidence. Criminals might overgeneralize from their experiences, leading them to adopt a skewed view of society, authority, or certain groups of people.

- **Magical Thinking**: Some criminals engage in magical thinking, an irrational belief that one's thoughts, words, or actions can influence events in a way that defies the laws of cause and effect. This can lead to a belief in being able to commit crimes without consequences.

- **Personalization and Egocentrism**: Personalization involves interpreting events as personally relevant or directed at oneself, often leading to misguided reactions. Egocentrism in criminals reflects a self-centered perspective where the impact of their actions on others is either ignored or grossly underestimated.

- **Catastrophizing**: This involves anticipating the worst possible outcome in a situation, often leading to excessive worry or risk-taking behaviors in an attempt to avoid these imagined scenarios.

Implications for Criminal Psychology

Understanding cognitive distortions in criminals is vital for several reasons. Firstly, it provides insights into the motivations behind criminal behavior, offering a window into how these individuals rationalize their actions. Secondly, it is crucial for the development of effective intervention strategies. Therapeutic approaches, such as cognitive-behavioral therapy, can help individuals recognize and challenge their distorted thoughts, leading to more rational and socially acceptable behavior patterns.

Psychopathy and ASPD

Psychopathy and Antisocial Personality Disorder (ASPD) are among the most extensively studied and discussed disorders. Both are characterized by a pattern of behavior that deviates markedly from societal norms and expectations, often leading to criminality. However, despite their similarities and frequent conflation in popular media, these disorders are distinct, each with unique characteristics and implications for understanding criminal behavior.

Psychopathy: Definition and Characteristics

Psychopathy is a complex personality disorder characterized by a range of affective, interpersonal, and behavioral traits. Key characteristics of psychopathy include:

- **Lack of Empathy and Remorse**: Psychopaths exhibit a profound lack of empathy for others, often unable to understand or care about the emotional states of other people. This is coupled with a lack of remorse or guilt for their actions, regardless of the harm they cause.

- **Superficial Charm and Manipulativeness**: Psychopaths are often articulate and superficially charming, adept at manipulation and deceit. This charm can be disarming, making it difficult for others to recognize their true intentions.

- **Egocentricity and Grandiosity**: A sense of superiority and grandiosity is common in psychopaths. They may have an inflated sense of self-worth and believe they are entitled to special treatment.

- **Impulsivity and Risk-Taking**: Psychopaths tend to be impulsive, taking risks without considering the consequences. This impulsivity often leads to problems with the law and engagement in criminal activities.

- **Shallow Affect**: Emotional depth is typically shallow in psychopaths. They may mimic emotions to manipulate others but lack genuine emotional experiences, particularly those related to attachment and fear.

Antisocial Personality Disorder (ASPD)

Antisocial Personality Disorder is a mental health condition characterized by a long-term pattern of disregarding or violating the rights of others. Key characteristics of ASPD include:

- **Disregard for Social Norms and Laws**: Individuals with ASPD often have a blatant disregard for societal norms and laws. They may repeatedly perform acts that are grounds for arrest, such as theft or violence.

- **Deceitfulness**: Lying, use of aliases, or conning others for personal profit or pleasure is common in individuals with ASPD.

- **Aggressiveness and Irritability**: People with ASPD may be irritable and aggressive, often getting into physical fights or assaults.

- **Reckless Disregard for Safety**: There is often a reckless disregard for the safety of themselves or others, leading to behavior that is potentially harmful.

- **Consistent Irresponsibility**: A failure to sustain consistent work behavior or honor financial obligations is often seen in those with ASPD.

Differentiating Psychopathy and ASPD

While psychopathy and ASPD share some overlapping traits, such as a disregard for societal norms and aggressive behavior, there are key differences:

- **Emotional Depth**: Psychopaths tend to have more significant emotional deficits, particularly in terms of empathy and remorse. Individuals with ASPD may still experience some level of empathy or remorse, albeit limited.

- **Social Functioning**: Psychopaths are often more adept at mimicking normal social behavior and can appear charming and trustworthy, unlike those with ASPD, who generally struggle more with social relationships.

- **Criminality**: While not all individuals with ASPD engage in criminal behavior, the disorder is more closely associated with criminality than psychopathy. Psychopaths, on the other hand, might engage in criminal acts more due to their manipulative and calculating nature.

Chapter Three: Development of Antisocial Behavior

The significance of early life experiences, particularly during childhood and adolescence, in shaping future behavior is increasingly recognized. These formative years are pivotal in the development of personality traits, coping mechanisms, and behavioral patterns.

The Impact of Early Childhood Experiences

The early years of a child's life are fundamental in laying the groundwork for future emotional, social, and cognitive development. During this period, several factors can significantly influence the likelihood of later criminal behavior:

- **Family Environment**: The family setting plays a crucial role in a child's development. Dysfunctional family dynamics, such as conflict, inconsistency in parenting styles, or lack of emotional support, can contribute to the development of behavioral issues. Conversely, a nurturing and stable family environment can act as a protective factor against future delinquency.

- **Exposure to Violence and Abuse**: Children who are exposed to violence, whether as direct victims or as witnesses, are at an increased risk of developing aggressive and antisocial behavior. Abuse, whether physical, emotional, or sexual, can have lasting impacts on a child's psychological well-being, often manifesting in harmful behaviors during adolescence and adulthood.

- **Early Behavioral Problems**: Signs of behavioral problems, such as aggression, defiance, and impulsivity, can emerge in early childhood. These early indicators, if not addressed, can escalate into more severe conduct problems and increase the risk of involvement in criminal activities.

- **Attachment and Bonding Issues**: Secure attachment to caregivers in early childhood is crucial for emotional regulation and social development. Disruptions in this attachment process, due to neglect or inconsistent caregiving, can lead to difficulties in forming healthy relationships and increase the likelihood of antisocial behavior.

Adolescent Development and Risk Factors

Adolescence is a period of significant change and development, marking the transition from childhood to adulthood. During this time, several factors can influence a young person's trajectory towards or away from criminal behavior:

- **Peer Influence**: Adolescents are particularly susceptible to peer influence. Association with delinquent peers can lead to the adoption of deviant behaviors and attitudes. Peer pressure can be a powerful force, leading adolescents to engage in activities they might otherwise avoid.

- **School Environment and Performance**: School experiences play a significant role in adolescent development. Academic failure, lack of engagement with school, and negative interactions with peers or teachers can contribute to delinquency. In contrast, a positive school environment can provide support and opportunities for constructive development.

- **Substance Use**: Experimentation with drugs and alcohol is more common in adolescence. Early substance use is a risk factor for a range of negative outcomes, including criminal behavior. It can impair judgment, increase impulsivity, and lead to the development of substance use disorders.

- **Mental Health Issues**: The onset of many mental health disorders occurs during adolescence. Conditions such as depression, anxiety, and conduct disorder can influence behavior and decision-making, potentially increasing the risk of criminal involvement.

The Interplay of Multiple Factors

It is important to recognize that no single factor determines criminal behavior. Rather, it is the interplay of multiple factors, often over an extended period, that influences an individual's pathway. Early adverse experiences can set the stage for later problems, but they do not doom a child to a life of criminality. Protective factors, such as supportive relationships, positive school experiences, and access to mental health services, can mitigate the impact of these risks.

The Impact of Familial Relationships

The impact of family dynamics and relationships on an individual's behavior is a subject of significant interest and importance. The family, as the primary unit of socialization, plays a pivotal role in shaping personality, behavior, and value systems.

The Role of Parenting Styles

Parenting styles have a profound impact on child development. Psychologists have identified several styles, each with different implications for a child's emotional and behavioral development:

- **Authoritative Parenting**: Characterized by a balance of responsiveness and demandingness, authoritative parenting is generally associated with positive behavioral outcomes. Children raised in such environments tend to exhibit lower levels of delinquency and antisocial behavior.

- **Authoritarian Parenting**: This style is high in demandingness but low in responsiveness. It often involves strict discipline and a lack of emotional warmth, which can lead to resentment, rebelliousness, and sometimes an inclination toward antisocial behavior.

- **Permissive Parenting**: Permissive parents are high in responsiveness but low in demandingness. This lack of structure and discipline can contribute to behavioral problems, including impulsivity and difficulties with authority.

- **Neglectful Parenting**: Neglectful or uninvolved parenting, characterized by a lack of responsiveness and demandingness, is often linked to the worst developmental outcomes. Children in these environments may seek attention and validation outside the family, sometimes in deviant peer groups, and engage in criminal behavior.

Family Structure and Its Impact

Family structure, including factors like single parenthood, divorce, or the presence of step-parents, can also influence a child's propensity for criminal behavior. While not deterministic, these factors can create stressors that affect family functioning and child development:

- **Single-Parent Families**: Children in single-parent families may face challenges such as economic hardship and reduced parental supervision, potentially increasing their vulnerability to engaging in delinquent behavior.

- **Divorce and Separation**: Divorce or separation can lead to emotional distress and behavioral issues in children. The degree of impact often depends on the level of conflict between parents, the quality of parenting post-divorce, and the child's ability to adapt to changes.

- **Stepfamilies**: Integrating into a stepfamily can be challenging for children. Difficulties in adjusting to new family dynamics and establishing relationships with stepparents can contribute to behavioral problems.

The Influence of Sibling Relationships

Siblings play a significant role in each other's lives, often serving as role models. In the context of criminal behavior, the influence of siblings can be particularly potent:

- **Modeling and Imitation**: Younger siblings may imitate the behavior of older siblings, including delinquent behavior. This imitation is more likely if the relationship is close and the older sibling is engaging in antisocial activities.

- **Sibling Rivalry and Conflict**: High levels of conflict and rivalry between siblings can lead to behavioral problems. In some cases, this can manifest as aggression or antisocial behavior.

Domestic Violence and Abuse

Exposure to domestic violence and experiencing abuse within the family are strong predictors of criminal behavior:

- **Witnessing Domestic Violence**: Children who witness domestic violence are at an increased risk of developing emotional and behavioral problems, including aggression and criminal behavior.

- **Physical and Emotional Abuse**: Abuse has long-term impacts on mental health and behavior. Victims of abuse are more likely to exhibit criminal behavior, partly as a coping mechanism or as a repetition of learned behavior.

How Societal Norms and Culture Shape Behavior

Social and cultural influences encompass a broad spectrum of factors, from societal norms and values to the cultural context in which an individual is raised and lives. These elements play a significant role in shaping attitudes, behaviors, and potentially, the propensity towards criminal behavior.

Societal Norms and Their Influence

Societal norms, the unwritten rules that govern behavior in a society, profoundly influence individual conduct. These norms dictate what is considered acceptable or unacceptable, shaping an individual's understanding of right and wrong.

- **Conformity and Deviance**: The pressure to conform to societal norms can be powerful. Deviance from these norms can lead to social sanctions, while adherence can result in acceptance and approval. When societal norms implicitly or explicitly endorse harmful behaviors or inequalities, they can contribute to criminal behavior.

- **Socialization and Learning**: The process of socialization, where individuals learn and internalize societal norms, plays a crucial role in shaping behavior. This learning happens through family, educational institutions, peer groups, and media. Inconsistent or harmful socialization can lead to the development of behaviors that are in conflict with legal norms.

Cultural Context and Its Impact

Culture, the shared beliefs, values, and practices of a group, also significantly influences behavior. Cultural context can shape an individual's attitudes towards authority, violence, and other behaviors relevant to criminal psychology.

- **Cultural Values**: Every culture has its own set of values that influence behavior. For example, cultures that value individualism may encourage self-reliance and personal achievement, sometimes at the expense of communal harmony or adherence to laws. Conversely, collectivist cultures may emphasize family and community cohesion, potentially discouraging behaviors that harm these social structures.

- **Subcultures and Crime**: Within larger societies, subcultures with distinct norms and values can exist. Some subcultures may have norms that conflict with those of the larger society, including the acceptance or even glorification of criminal behavior. This can be particularly influential during adolescence, a time when peer group and subcultural influences are strong.

Influence of Socioeconomic Factors

Socioeconomic factors, deeply intertwined with social and cultural context, also play a role in shaping behavior.

- **Poverty and Inequality**: Socioeconomic disadvantages, such as poverty and inequality, can increase the likelihood of criminal behavior. Economic strain can lead to engagement in illegal activities as a means of survival or as a response to perceived injustices.

- **Access to Resources**: Limited access to education, employment opportunities, and social services in economically disadvantaged areas can contribute to criminal behavior. These limitations can lead to a sense of hopelessness or frustration, potentially driving individuals toward illegal activities as a means of coping or advancement.

Media and Technological Influences

In the modern world, media and technology significantly impact societal norms and behaviors.

- **Media Representation**: The portrayal of violence, crime, and justice in media can influence public perceptions and attitudes. Media can normalize certain behaviors or attitudes, potentially impacting real-world behavior and choices.

- **Digital Culture**: The rise of digital culture and online communities has created new spaces where social and cultural norms are formed and disseminated. These online spaces can sometimes foster harmful behaviors, including cyberbullying, online radicalization, or the spread of criminal ideologies.

Substance Abuse and Antisocial Behavior

The relationship between substance abuse and antisocial behavior is complex and multifaceted, involving a range of psychological, social, and biological factors.

Defining the Relationship

Substance abuse refers to the harmful or hazardous use of psychoactive substances, including alcohol and illicit drugs. Antisocial behavior, on the other hand, is characterized by actions that are hostile, harmful, or violate social norms and the rights of others. The relationship between these two phenomena is often reciprocal and bidirectional.

The Role of Substance Abuse in Antisocial Behavior

- **Disinhibition**: Substance abuse can lead to disinhibition, where an individual's ability to restrain impulses is diminished. This can result in an increased likelihood of engaging in risky or aggressive behaviors that are characteristic of antisocial personality patterns.

- **Impaired Judgment and Decision-Making**: The use of substances can impair judgment and decision-making abilities, leading to poor choices and actions that defy social norms and laws.

- **Escalation of Pre-existing Tendencies**: In individuals with pre-existing antisocial tendencies, substance abuse can exacerbate these behaviors. It can serve as a catalyst, increasing the frequency or severity of antisocial acts.

- **Criminal Activities Associated with Substance Abuse**: The need to sustain a substance abuse habit can drive individuals to engage in criminal activities such as theft, drug dealing, or prostitution. These activities are often accompanied by additional antisocial behaviors.

The Impact of Antisocial Behavior on Substance Abuse

- **Coping Mechanism**: For some individuals, substance abuse may be a coping mechanism for dealing with the consequences or the internal experience of antisocial behavior, leading to a cycle where each reinforces the other.

- **Social and Peer Influences**: Antisocial behavior is often associated with social environments where substance abuse is normalized. Peer influence can play a significant role in the initiation and continuation of substance use.

- **Rebellion Against Norms**: In some cases, both substance abuse and antisocial behavior can be forms of rebellion against societal norms and authority figures, particularly in adolescents and young adults.

Biological and Genetic Factors

Research indicates that there may be genetic and biological factors that predispose individuals to both substance abuse and antisocial behavior.

- **Genetic Predisposition**: Studies suggest that there may be genetic components that increase susceptibility to both substance abuse and antisocial behavior, although the exact nature of these genetic factors is complex and not fully understood.

- **Neurobiological Factors**: Neurobiological research has shown that certain brain structures and neurotransmitter systems are implicated in both substance abuse and antisocial behavior, suggesting a shared physiological basis.

Social and Environmental Factors

The social and environmental context in which an individual lives can significantly influence the likelihood of both substance abuse and antisocial behavior.

- **Family Dynamics**: Dysfunctional family environments, including exposure to substance abuse and antisocial behavior within the family, can increase the risk of these behaviors in offspring.

- **Socioeconomic Status**: Lower socioeconomic status and associated stressors can contribute to higher rates of substance abuse and antisocial behavior.

Prevention and Intervention Strategies to Curb Antisocial Tendencies

Addressing antisocial tendencies through early intervention is a key area of focus in criminal psychology. The goal is to identify and modify risk factors and behaviors before they solidify into more serious antisocial or criminal patterns. This proactive approach involves a spectrum of strategies, from family-based interventions to community and school programs, aiming to alter the developmental trajectory that could lead to criminal behavior.

Early interventions are crucial because behavioral patterns established in childhood and adolescence can have long-lasting effects. Intervening during these formative years offers the best chance to redirect potentially harmful trajectories. It also helps in addressing the root causes of behavior rather than merely its symptoms.

Family-Centered Interventions

- **Parent Training Programs**: These programs focus on teaching effective parenting skills, including communication, discipline, and nurturing practices. The goal is to foster a supportive family environment that promotes healthy development and mitigates risk factors for antisocial behavior.

- **Family Therapy**: This involves working with the entire family to improve communication, solve problems, and address specific issues that may contribute to a child's antisocial behavior. This can be particularly effective in cases where family conflict or dysfunction is a contributing factor.

School-Based Interventions

- **Social and Emotional Learning (SEL) Programs**: These programs are implemented in schools to teach children skills like empathy, problem-solving, emotional regulation, and responsible decision-making. SEL programs aim to promote a positive school climate and reduce behavior problems.

- **Bullying Prevention Programs**: Bullying is both a symptom and a risk factor for antisocial behavior. School-based interventions that target bullying can help in creating a safe and inclusive environment, reducing the likelihood of developing antisocial tendencies.

Community-Based Programs

- **Mentorship Programs**: Pairing at-risk youth with positive role models can provide them with guidance, support, and opportunities to develop new skills and interests. These relationships can offer a positive influence, countering risk factors present in other areas of a youth's life.

- **After-School and Recreational Programs**: Providing structured and supervised activities after school can keep children and adolescents engaged in constructive activities, reducing the likelihood of involvement in antisocial behavior and providing opportunities for social development.

Individual-Focused Interventions

- **Cognitive-Behavioral Therapy (CBT)**: CBT is effective in helping individuals recognize and alter negative thought patterns and behaviors. It can be used to address specific issues such as aggression, impulse control, and substance abuse.

- **Skill Development**: Interventions focusing on skill development, such as anger management, conflict resolution, and communication skills, can equip individuals with the tools needed to manage and express emotions in a healthy way.

Integrating Multi-Systemic Approaches

Effective intervention often requires a multi-systemic approach, which involves coordinating efforts across family, schools, and the community. This ensures a comprehensive support system that addresses various aspects of a child's life.

Prevention Programs and Public Policy

Prevention programs, supported by public policy, can play a significant role in addressing broader societal factors that contribute to antisocial behavior. Policies aimed at reducing poverty, improving access to education and mental health services, and fostering community development can help mitigate some of the root causes of antisocial behavior.

Chapter Four: Crime Typologies

Motives and Psychology Behind Violence

Violent crimes, characterized by the use or threat of physical force, are a significant area of study within criminal psychology. Violent crimes encompass a range of actions, including homicide, assault, robbery, sexual violence, and domestic abuse. These crimes can vary greatly in terms of severity, context, and impact on victims and society.

Psychological Motives Behind Violence

- **Power and Control**: One of the primary motives behind many violent crimes is the desire for power and control. Perpetrators may use violence as a means to dominate and assert control over their victims, often stemming from feelings of powerlessness or inadequacy in other areas of their lives.

- **Retaliation and Revenge**: Violence is often used as a tool for retaliation or revenge. This can be motivated by real or perceived injustices, where the perpetrator seeks to punish those they believe have wronged them.

- **Fear and Self-Defense**: In some cases, violent behavior is driven by fear and a perceived need for self-defense. This may be seen in situations where individuals feel threatened and believe violence is necessary to protect themselves.

- **Anger and Frustration**: Uncontrolled anger and frustration can escalate into violent behavior. This is often the result of accumulated stressors, where violence becomes an outlet for expressing and relieving these intense emotions.

- **Mental Health Issues**: Certain mental health disorders, including some personality disorders and psychotic disorders, can increase the risk of violent behavior. However, it is essential to note that mental illness is not a direct cause of violence, and most individuals with mental health issues are not violent.

Psychological Profiles of Violent Offenders

Understanding the psychological profiles of violent offenders is key to understanding the motives behind their actions.

- **Antisocial Personality Traits**: Individuals who commit violent crimes often exhibit traits associated with antisocial personality disorder, such as impulsivity, a lack of empathy, and disregard for the rights of others.

- **History of Abuse or Trauma**: Many violent offenders have histories of abuse or trauma. Childhood experiences of physical, sexual, or emotional abuse can contribute to the development of violent behavior in adulthood.

- **Substance Abuse**: Substance abuse can exacerbate existing tendencies towards violence or lower inhibitions, making violent outbursts more likely.

Environmental and Cultural Factors

The environment in which an individual is raised and lives can significantly impact their propensity for violence.

- **Family Environment**: A family history of violence, poor parental supervision, and dysfunctional family dynamics can contribute to the development of violent behavior.

- **Socioeconomic Factors**: Poverty, lack of education, and exposure to crime-ridden neighborhoods can create conditions that foster violent behavior.

- **Cultural Norms**: Cultural norms that glorify or normalize violence can contribute to the acceptance and perpetration of violent acts.

Prevention and Intervention

Preventing and intervening in cases of violent crime require a multifaceted approach.

- **Early Intervention**: Addressing risk factors in childhood, such as abuse, neglect, and behavioral problems, is crucial for preventing the development of violent behavior.

- **Therapeutic Interventions**: Psychological interventions, such as anger management, cognitive-behavioral therapy, and trauma-informed care, can be effective in treating individuals prone to violence.

- **Community Programs**: Community-based programs that provide support, education, and resources can help mitigate the environmental and socioeconomic factors that contribute to violence.

Sexual Offenses

These crimes are particularly distressing due to their intimate nature and the profound impact they have on victims. Sexual offenders are not a homogeneous group, making it challenging to generalize their psychological profiles. However, there are certain commonalities in psychological factors and patterns that can be identified.

- **Cognitive Distortions**: Many sexual offenders exhibit cognitive distortions related to sex and relationships. These may include beliefs that minimize the harm caused to victims, entitlement to sex, or misconceptions about the nature of consent. Such distortions justify their actions in their own minds.

- **Empathy Deficits**: A lack of empathy, particularly towards victims, is a common trait among sexual offenders. This lack of empathy is often what allows them to commit offenses without regard for the impact on their victims.

- **Poor Impulse Control**: Impulsivity and poor behavioral control can contribute to the commission of sexual offenses. This may be compounded by substance abuse, which further impairs judgment and self-control.

- **Sexual Preoccupation and Deviant Sexual Interests**: Some offenders exhibit a high degree of sexual preoccupation or have specific deviant sexual interests. These interests, especially when coupled with poor impulse control and cognitive distortions, can increase the risk of committing sexual offenses.

- **History of Abuse and Trauma**: A history of sexual or physical abuse in childhood is noted in some sexual offenders. This early exposure to sexualized behavior or violence can sometimes play a role in the development of harmful sexual behaviors in adulthood.

- **Social and Relational Deficits**: Difficulties in forming healthy, adult relationships can be seen in some offenders. These deficits can lead to a reliance on coercion or manipulation to achieve sexual gratification.

The Role of Power and Control

Sexual offenses are often less about sexual gratification and more about power and control. Offenders may use sexual violence as a means to dominate and exert power over their victims. This can be particularly evident in cases of serial rape or sexually motivated homicides.

The Impact of Societal and Cultural Factors

Societal attitudes towards sex and gender can also influence the prevalence and nature of sexual offenses. Cultural norms that objectify women or promote toxic masculinity can contribute to attitudes and behaviors that condone or normalize sexual violence.

Prevention and Intervention

Understanding the psychological underpinnings of sexual offenses is key to developing effective prevention and intervention strategies.

- **Risk Assessment**: Identifying individuals at high risk of committing sexual offenses is crucial. This involves evaluating factors like past behavior, psychological traits, and environmental influences.

- **Treatment Programs**: Treatment for sexual offenders often includes addressing cognitive distortions, developing empathy, and managing sexual arousal or deviant interests. Cognitive-behavioral therapy and relapse prevention strategies are commonly used.

- **Community Education**: Public education campaigns that address issues like consent, respectful relationships, and bystander intervention can play a role in preventing sexual offenses.

- **Policy and Legal Frameworks**: Robust legal frameworks and policies that address sexual violence, protect victims, and provide clear consequences for offenders are essential.

White-Collar Crimes

White-collar crimes, characterized by deceit, concealment, or violation of trust for financial gain, are a distinct category of criminal activity. White-collar crime typically involves illegal activities committed by individuals in their professional capacity. Common examples include fraud, embezzlement, insider trading, tax evasion, and money laundering. These crimes are often complex and can span years, involving sophisticated schemes and manipulation of information.

Psychological Traits and Mindsets

- **Rationalization and Justification**: A key feature of the white-collar criminal mindset is the ability to rationalize and justify illegal actions. Offenders often view their actions as a necessary means to an end, or as not truly harmful. This rationalization can be supported by beliefs that their actions are for the greater good, or that they are entitled to the fruits of their deceit due to their hard work or intelligence.

- **Sense of Entitlement and Superiority**: Many white-collar criminals exhibit a sense of entitlement or superiority. They may believe that their status or intelligence justifies bending or breaking the rules. This can be compounded by environments where success and wealth are highly valued, and ethical considerations are secondary.

- **Greed and Materialism**: Greed is a significant motivator in many white-collar crimes. The desire for wealth, power, and status can drive individuals to engage in illegal activities, especially in cultures that value material success.

- **Thrill-Seeking and Risk-Taking**: For some, the thrill of outsmarting the system or getting away with deceit can be a motivating factor. This risk-taking behavior is often accompanied by a belief in their own ability to avoid detection.

- **Lack of Empathy and Disregard for Impact**: White-collar criminals often exhibit a lack of empathy for those affected by their actions. The impersonal nature of their crimes can make it easier to ignore the broader impacts on individuals, companies, or the economy.

The Role of Environmental and Cultural Factors

The environment in which individuals operate can significantly influence the likelihood of engaging in white-collar crime.

- **Corporate Culture and Peer Influence**: A corporate culture that implicitly or explicitly encourages rule-bending for the sake of success can foster white-collar crime. Peer influence and the normalization of unethical behavior in professional settings can further exacerbate this risk.

- **Opportunity and Rationalization**: Access to large sums of money and complex financial systems can provide both the opportunity and the means to commit white-collar crimes. The complexity and perceived victimlessness of these crimes can make them easier to rationalize.

- **Regulatory Environment**: Weak regulatory environments or the perception of lax enforcement can increase the temptation to engage in white-collar crime, as the perceived risk of getting caught is low.

Prevention and Intervention

Addressing white-collar crime requires a multifaceted approach that includes stricter regulations, corporate culture changes, and targeted interventions.

- **Strengthening Regulations and Enforcement**: Effective regulatory frameworks and diligent enforcement are essential to deter white-collar crime. This includes harsher penalties for offenders and improved oversight mechanisms.

- **Ethical Corporate Culture**: Promoting an ethical corporate culture, where success is not achieved at the expense of legality and ethics, is crucial. This involves leadership that models ethical behavior and systems that reward integrity.

- **Education and Training**: Providing education and training on ethical decision-making, legal compliance, and the consequences of white-collar crime can help prevent these offenses.

Organized Crime

Organized crime refers to crimes committed by structured groups systematically and persistently, often for monetary gain. These groups engage in various illegal activities, including drug trafficking, human trafficking, money laundering, and extortion. The structure and hierarchy of these organizations often mirror legitimate businesses, with defined roles and responsibilities. Unlike impulsive or solitary criminals, members of organized crime syndicates often exhibit specific psychological characteristics that facilitate their involvement in and perpetuation of coordinated criminal activities.

Psychological Traits

- **Loyalty and Solidarity**: Loyalty to the group is a predominant trait among members of organized crime networks. This loyalty is often cultivated through shared experiences, rituals, and the notion of a "code of honor." The solidarity among members is pivotal for the group's survival and effectiveness.

- **Risk-Taking and Thrill-Seeking**: Individuals involved in organized crime often exhibit risk-taking behaviors. This trait is not merely about seeking thrills but also about a calculated approach to risk, weighing potential gains against the dangers involved.

- **Pragmatism and Strategic Thinking**: Unlike impulsive criminals, members of organized crime networks tend to be more pragmatic and strategic. They are often involved in planning and executing complex schemes, requiring a level of foresight and tactical thinking.

- **Ability to Rationalize and Justify**: Individuals in these groups are adept at rationalizing their involvement in criminal activities. They often justify their actions as a means of survival, as loyalty to their "family," or as a necessary evil in a corrupt world.

- **Desensitization to Violence**: Exposure to and participation in violent acts can lead to desensitization. This trait is crucial for carrying out some of the more ruthless aspects of organized crime without hesitation or remorse.

- **Adaptability and Resilience**: The clandestine and often volatile nature of organized crime requires individuals to be adaptable and resilient. They must navigate complex legal and illegal environments, constantly adjusting to new challenges and threats.

- **Charisma and Leadership Skills**: Leaders of organized crime groups often possess charisma and strong leadership skills, enabling them to inspire loyalty and manage large networks of individuals. These skills are essential for maintaining order and cohesion within the group.

The Role of Environmental and Social Factors

The decision to join and remain in an organized crime network is often influenced by environmental and social factors.

- **Socioeconomic Background**: Many individuals in organized crime come from impoverished or marginalized communities, where opportunities for legal advancement are limited. Organized crime can offer a means of economic and social advancement.

- **Cultural and Familial Influence**: In some cases, involvement in organized crime is a family tradition or a cultural norm, with younger generations following in the footsteps of older family members.

- **The Appeal of Power and Status**: The allure of power, respect, and financial gain can be powerful motivators for joining organized crime. For some, the prestige associated with being part of a feared and respected organization is a significant draw.

Cybercrime

Cybercrime, a relatively new and evolving domain of criminal activity, represents a significant challenge. Unlike traditional crimes, cybercrime is characterized by its virtual nature, spanning activities like hacking, online fraud, identity theft, cyberbullying, and illegal content distribution. The anonymous and remote nature of these crimes sets them apart from traditional criminal activities.

Psychological Traits and Motivations

- **Anonymity and Disinhibition**: The anonymity afforded by the internet can lead to a sense of disinhibition among cybercriminals. This often results in them engaging in activities they might not consider in a face-to-face context.

- **Technical Skill and Intelligence**: Many forms of cybercrime require a high level of technical skill and intelligence. Cybercriminals often have extensive knowledge of computer systems, networks, and programming.

- **Thrill-Seeking and Challenge**: For some cybercriminals, the thrill of breaking into secure systems or outsmarting security measures is a significant motivator. The challenge and excitement of engaging in these activities can be addictive.

- **Lack of Empathy and Rationalization**: Similar to traditional criminals, cybercriminals often display a lack of empathy for their victims. They may rationalize their behavior by perceiving their actions as victimless crimes, especially in cases of hacking or financial fraud.

- **Greed and Financial Gain**: Financial gain is a major motivator for many cybercriminals, particularly in activities like online fraud, identity theft, and extortion.

- **Social and Ideological Motives**: Some cybercriminals are driven by social or ideological motives. This includes hackers who engage in activities for political reasons (hacktivism) or to expose perceived injustices.

The Role of Social and Environmental Factors

The decision to engage in cybercrime is often influenced by social and environmental factors, including:

- **Online Communities and Peer Influence**: Participation in certain online communities can influence individuals to engage in or rationalize cybercriminal behavior. Peer influence in these communities can be significant, particularly for younger individuals.

- **Cultural and Societal Norms**: Societal attitudes towards technology, privacy, and internet behavior can impact the prevalence and nature of cybercrime. In cultures where internet laws are lax or not well-enforced, cybercrime might be more rampant.

- **Opportunity and Accessibility**: The widespread availability of internet access and the relative ease of engaging in cybercriminal activities, compared to traditional crimes, make it an accessible option for many.

Challenges in Addressing Cybercrime

Addressing cybercrime presents unique challenges, including:

- **Detection and Prosecution Difficulties**: The anonymity and transnational nature of cybercrime make it difficult to detect, trace, and prosecute offenders.

- **Evolving Nature of the Crime**: The rapid pace of technological advancement means that cybercrime is continually evolving, requiring constant adaptation of prevention and enforcement strategies.

- **Psychological Impact on Victims**: Cybercrimes can have a significant psychological impact on victims, including feelings of violation, fear, and helplessness. This is particularly true in cases of cyberbullying or online harassment.

Prevention and Intervention

Preventing cybercrime involves a combination of technological solutions, legal frameworks, and psychological interventions, such as:

- **Cybersecurity Education**: Educating the public about safe online practices is crucial in preventing cybercrime.

- **Legal and Regulatory Frameworks**: Strong laws and international cooperation are required to combat cybercrime effectively.

- **Psychological Profiling and Intervention**: Understanding the psychological profiles of cybercriminals can aid in developing targeted intervention strategies. This includes addressing the underlying motivations and providing alternatives to those at risk of engaging in cybercrime.

Chapter Five: Victimology

Understanding the experience and psychological impact on victims of crime is as crucial as studying the offenders. Being a victim of a crime, whether it's a violent offense, a theft, or a personal violation like fraud, can have profound and lasting psychological effects. These impacts vary widely depending on the individual, the nature of the crime, and the support received afterward.

The Immediate Psychological Impact

The immediate aftermath of being a victim can involve a range of intense emotional responses:

- **Shock and Disbelief**: Initially, victims often experience shock and disbelief, struggling to comprehend that the crime has occurred. This can be accompanied by numbness or detachment as the mind attempts to process the traumatic event.

- **Fear and Anxiety**: Fear is a common response, particularly if the crime was violent or invasive. Victims may fear for their safety, the safety of loved ones, or fear a recurrence of the crime. This can lead to heightened anxiety and hypervigilance.

- **Anger and Frustration**: Anger towards the perpetrator is natural, as is frustration with the situation or with the criminal justice system, especially if the victim feels that their case is not being handled adequately.

- **Shame and Guilt**: Victims may irrationally blame themselves for the crime, leading to feelings of shame or guilt. This is especially prevalent in cases of sexual assault or domestic abuse.

Long-Term Psychological Effects

The long-term psychological impact of being a crime victim can be far-reaching:

- **Post-Traumatic Stress Disorder (PTSD)**: Many crime victims experience symptoms of PTSD, such as flashbacks, nightmares, severe anxiety, and uncontrollable thoughts about the event.

- **Depression and Withdrawal**: Prolonged emotional distress can lead to depression. Victims might withdraw from social interactions, lose interest in activities they once enjoyed, or experience a persistent sense of sadness.

- **Trust Issues and Relationship Struggles**: Experiencing a crime can lead to difficulties trusting others, which can strain personal relationships. Victims might find it hard to form new relationships or maintain existing ones.

- **Changes in Personality and Behavior**: Some victims may undergo noticeable changes in personality or behavior. They may become more cautious, aggressive, or change their lifestyle or habits significantly.

Coping and Resilience

Victims' responses to crime vary greatly, and resilience plays a key role:

- **Coping Mechanisms**: Each victim copes differently; some might find strength in seeking justice, others in connecting with loved ones or through professional counseling. Healthy coping mechanisms are crucial for recovery.

- **Support Systems**: The presence of a strong support system, including family, friends, and professional assistance, can greatly influence the victim's ability to cope and recover.

- **Resilience Factors**: Individual factors such as pre-existing mental health, past experiences, and personal resilience impact how a victim processes and recovers from the crime.

Role of Criminal Justice System and Society

The criminal justice system and societal reactions play a significant role in the victim's psychological journey:

- **Justice and Closure**: The process of seeking justice, whether through legal means or through restorative justice approaches, can provide a sense of closure and empowerment for some victims.

- **Victim Blaming and Stigmatization**: Societal attitudes can significantly impact a victim's psychological well-being. Victim-blaming attitudes or stigmatization can exacerbate feelings of guilt and shame.

- **Victim Assistance Programs**: Access to victim assistance programs, counseling, and support groups can aid in the recovery process, providing necessary resources and support.

Victim-Offender Relationships

The dynamics between victims and offenders in criminal psychology are multifaceted. These relationships can vary greatly depending on the nature of the crime, the backgrounds of the individuals involved, and the circumstances under which the crime occurred.

Types of Victim-Offender Relationships

- **Stranger Crimes**: In many crimes, the victim and offender do not know each other prior to the criminal act. Such situations can include random acts of violence, theft, or cybercrime. The impersonal nature of these crimes can affect how victims process the trauma and how offenders rationalize their actions.

- **Acquaintance Crimes**: Often, crimes are committed by someone the victim knows, such as a neighbor, colleague, or friend. These crimes can lead to a profound sense of betrayal for the victim, complicating the emotional and psychological impact.

- **Intimate Partner and Domestic Crimes**: Crimes committed within intimate relationships, including domestic violence and sexual assault, are among the most psychologically complex. The intertwined nature of affection and abuse creates a complicated dynamic, often characterized by power imbalances and emotional manipulation.

- **Family-Related Crimes**: Crimes involving family members, such as child abuse or elder abuse, entail a significant breach of trust and care, deeply affecting the victim's psychological well-being and perception of familial relationships.

Psychological Impact and Dynamics

- **Power and Control**: Many crimes, especially those in intimate or familial relationships, involve an element of power and control. Offenders may use the crime as a means to exert power over the victim, leading to long-term psychological impacts such as fear, helplessness, and loss of autonomy.

- **Manipulation and Coercion**: In some relationships, particularly in cases of domestic abuse or exploitation, the offender may use manipulation or coercion to control the victim. This can lead to complex emotional responses, including guilt, shame, and conflicted feelings towards the offender.

- **Trauma Bonding**: In prolonged abusive situations, victims can develop trauma bonds with their abusers, characterized by loyalty or affection in the context of abuse. This bond can be particularly challenging to break and can complicate recovery and intervention efforts.

- **Retaliation and Fear of Reporting**: Fear of retaliation or further harm can be a significant factor in victim-offender dynamics, especially if the offender holds a position of power or influence. This fear can deter victims from reporting the crime or seeking help.

Impact on Rehabilitation and Legal Proceedings

- **Restorative Justice Approaches**: In some cases, especially where the victim and offender have an ongoing relationship, restorative justice approaches can be effective. These approaches focus on repairing the harm caused by the crime and can involve mediated encounters between the victim and offender.

- **Impact on Sentencing and Legal Outcomes**: The nature of the victim-offender relationship can influence legal proceedings and sentencing. In cases of domestic violence or child abuse, for instance, the court may consider the breach of trust as an aggravating factor.

- **Support Services for Victims**: Understanding the dynamics of victim-offender relationships is crucial for providing appropriate support services to victims. This includes tailored counseling, legal assistance, and safety planning, especially in ongoing or intimate relationships.

How Offenders Choose Their Victims

Victim selection is a process often influenced by specific vulnerabilities perceived by the offender, and can vary greatly depending on the type of crime and the individual committing it. Delving into this aspect offers significant insights into the criminal mind and behavior.

Factors Influencing Victim Selection

- **Perceived Vulnerability**: Offenders often choose victims based on perceived vulnerability. This can include physical vulnerability, such as choosing victims who are physically weaker or less able to defend themselves, as well as psychological or emotional vulnerability, like individuals who appear more trusting or naïve.

- **Opportunity and Accessibility**: The opportunity to commit the crime often plays a significant role in victim selection. Offenders may target individuals who are readily accessible or in a situation where the offender can easily approach them, such as isolated locations or via online platforms.

- **Desirability Based on Offender's Motivation**: Depending on the motivation behind the crime, offenders might look for specific characteristics in their victims. For instance, in sexually motivated crimes, the offender's specific preferences will play a role. In financial crimes, individuals with perceived wealth or access to financial resources might be targeted.

- **Anonymity and Risk Assessment**: Offenders often choose victims based on how likely they are to be caught. This can include targeting strangers over acquaintances or choosing victims in situations where the crime can be committed anonymously or with a lower risk of identification.

- **Repeat Victimization**: In some cases, offenders may target individuals who have been victimized before, as they may perceive these individuals as less likely to report the crime or be believed.

Psychological Traits of Offenders and Victim Selection

- **Power and Control Dynamics**: In crimes like domestic violence or sexual assault, the selection of a victim is often about power and control. The offender may choose victims they perceive as being more submissive or less likely to fight back.

- **Fantasy and Idealization**: Particularly in sexually motivated crimes, offenders might select victims based on a specific fantasy or idealization. This can be influenced by personal desires, cultural or societal norms, or other psychological factors.

- **Cognitive Distortions and Rationalizations**: Offenders often use cognitive distortions to rationalize their choice of victims. They might convince themselves that the victim deserved it, was a willing participant, or wouldn't be harmed by the crime.

Social and Cultural Influences

- **Socially Constructed Vulnerabilities**: Societal norms and stereotypes can influence perceptions of vulnerability. For example, women and children are often stereotypically viewed as more vulnerable, making them more likely targets for certain types of crime.

- **Cultural and Environmental Context**: The cultural and environmental context in which both the offender and potential victim exist can influence victim selection. This includes factors like social norms, community structure, and the level of surveillance or security in an area.

Implications for Prevention and Law Enforcement

- **Risk Reduction and Awareness**: Understanding how offenders select victims can inform strategies to reduce risk and raise awareness among potential target groups.

- **Profiling and Investigative Strategies**: Insights into victim selection can aid law enforcement in profiling offenders and predicting future targets, which can be crucial in preventing further crimes and apprehending perpetrators.

- **Victim Support Services**: Recognizing patterns in victim selection can help in providing targeted support services to those most at risk of certain crimes.

Secondary Victimization

Secondary victimization refers to the additional trauma experienced by crime victims as a result of the responses of institutions and individuals with whom they interact following the primary victimization. This concept highlights how societal and systemic factors can exacerbate the distress experienced by victims. Secondary victimization can occur through various means, including the criminal justice system, medical institutions, media, social networks, and community reactions. It often involves victim-blaming attitudes, lack of support, re-traumatization, and insensitivity to the victim's experience.

Sources and Forms of Secondary Victimization

- **The Criminal Justice System**: The procedures and interactions within the criminal justice system can contribute to secondary victimization. This can include insensitive questioning, disbelief or skepticism about the victim's account, prolonged legal processes, and lack of information or support throughout the legal proceedings.

- **Medical and Support Services**: Inadequate care or insensitive treatment by medical professionals and support workers can further traumatize victims. This includes lack of privacy, forced retelling of traumatic events without psychological support, and lack of empathy in service provision.

- **Media Representation**: Media coverage of crimes can lead to secondary victimization, especially when it involves sensationalism, invasion of privacy, or portrayal of the victim in a negative light. The focus on lurid details rather than the victim's experience can be particularly damaging.

- **Social and Community Reactions**: Victim-blaming attitudes, stigma, or lack of support from family, friends, and the community can exacerbate the trauma experienced by victims. Social isolation and ostracism are common forms of secondary victimization.

- **Workplace and Educational Settings**: Lack of support or understanding in workplaces and educational institutions, such as forced leave, discrimination, or gossip, can also contribute to secondary victimization.

Psychological Impact of Secondary Victimization

- **Exacerbation of Trauma**: Secondary victimization can exacerbate the initial trauma, leading to heightened symptoms of post-traumatic stress, anxiety, and depression.

- **Erosion of Trust**: Experiences of secondary victimization often lead to a loss of trust in institutions and society, which can hinder the victim's recovery and willingness to seek help.

- **Reduced Reporting**: Fear of secondary victimization can deter victims from reporting crimes or seeking help, leading to underreporting of certain types of crimes, particularly sexual assault and domestic violence.

Systemic and Societal Implications

- **Legal and Institutional Reforms**: There is a need for reforms in legal and institutional practices to minimize secondary victimization. This includes training for professionals in handling victims sensitively, victim-centered approaches in legal proceedings, and improved support services.

- **Public Awareness and Education**: Raising public awareness about the impact of secondary victimization and promoting a culture of support and understanding for victims are essential steps in addressing this issue.

- **Policy Development**: Developing policies that prioritize the mental health and wellbeing of victims in all interactions post-crime is crucial. This involves multidisciplinary coordination between law enforcement, medical services, mental health professionals, and victim support organizations.

Support and Recovery for Victims

Victims of crime can experience a wide range of psychological effects, including trauma, anxiety, depression, and post-traumatic stress disorder (PTSD). The nature and extent of these effects often depend on factors such as the type of crime, the victim's previous experiences, and their personal coping mechanisms. Providing effective psychological support to victims is paramount in helping them to heal and regain a sense of safety and normalcy in their lives. This support comes in various forms and is tailored to address the unique needs and experiences of each victim.

Types of Psychological Support for Victims

- **Crisis Intervention**: Immediately following a crime, victims may require crisis intervention services. This short-term assistance focuses on stabilizing their emotional state and providing immediate support and information. Crisis intervention can be provided through hotlines, emergency shelters, or emergency counseling services.

- **Trauma-Informed Therapy**: For longer-term treatment, trauma-informed therapy is crucial. This therapy acknowledges the impact of trauma on a victim's life and helps them process their experiences in a safe, supportive environment. Techniques may include cognitive-behavioral therapy (CBT), eye movement desensitization and reprocessing (EMDR), or narrative therapy.

- **Group Therapy and Support Groups**: Group therapy and support groups can be beneficial for victims, providing a space to share experiences and coping strategies with others who have been through similar situations. These groups offer solidarity and understanding, which can be powerful in the healing process.

- **Family Therapy**: For some victims, family therapy may be necessary, especially if the crime has affected the entire family or if family dynamics contribute to the victim's stress. This therapy focuses on improving communication, understanding the impact of the crime on the family, and strengthening family support systems.

- **Psychoeducation**: Educating victims about the psychological effects of being a victim of crime is an important aspect of support. Understanding their reactions and emotions can be empowering for victims and can aid in the recovery process.

- **Empowerment and Skill Building**: Helping victims develop skills to regain control over their lives is a critical component of recovery. This can include self-defense training, assertiveness training, or skill-building for coping with anxiety and stress.

Systemic and Community Support

- **Victim Assistance Programs**: Many communities have victim assistance programs that provide a range of services, including legal assistance, advocacy, and counseling. These programs are designed to help victims navigate the aftermath of a crime.

- **Community Resources**: Community resources such as crisis centers, hotlines, and shelters play a vital role in providing immediate and ongoing support to victims.

- **Integrating Support Services**: Effective support for victims often requires coordination between various services, including mental health professionals, law enforcement, legal services, and community organizations. Integrated care ensures that victims receive comprehensive support tailored to their needs.

Challenges in Victim Support

- **Access to Services**: Ensuring that victims have access to the support they need is a significant challenge. Barriers can include lack of awareness of available services, geographical limitations, and financial constraints.

- **Cultural and Linguistic Appropriateness**: Providing support that is culturally sensitive and in the victim's language is crucial for effective therapy and assistance.

- **Continuity of Care**: For some victims, long-term support may be necessary. Ensuring continuity of care and ongoing access to mental health services is essential for sustained recovery.

Chapter Six: The Art of Profiling

Criminal profiling involves the construction of a psychological, behavioral, and demographic profile of an unknown offender based on the characteristics of the crime. Criminal profiling is grounded in the understanding that behavior reflects personality. By examining how a crime is committed, profilers infer the characteristics, beliefs, and social practices of the perpetrator. This process is based on the analysis of the crime scene, victimology, and the details of the crime itself.

Steps in Criminal Profiling

- **Data Collection and Analysis**: The first step involves gathering all available information about the crime. This includes crime scene photographs, autopsy reports, witness statements, and police reports. The profiler analyzes this data to understand the sequence of events, the nature of the crime, and the interaction between the offender and the victim.

- **Crime Scene Classification**: Crime scenes are typically classified as organized or disorganized. An organized crime scene suggests a perpetrator who plans the crime, exercises control, and leaves few clues. A disorganized crime scene indicates an impulsive, chaotic perpetrator, possibly with underlying mental health issues.

- **Victimology**: Profilers study the victim(s) to understand why they might have been targeted. This includes examining their lifestyle, background, and the nature of their interactions with the offender.

- **Offender Characteristics**: Based on the analysis, a profile is developed outlining the likely characteristics of the offender. This can include age range, employment, psychological characteristics, living arrangements, and even possible physical features.

- **Apprehension Strategy**: The profile is used to guide law enforcement in narrowing down suspects and developing strategies for apprehension.

Theoretical Foundations of Profiling

Criminal profiling is rooted in several psychological theories and principles:

- **Behavioral Consistency**: The principle that individuals are consistent in their behavior across different situations. This consistency allows profilers to predict future actions of the offender based on past behaviors.

- **Psychological Theories**: Various psychological theories, including personality theories and psychopathology, inform the practice of profiling. Understanding mental disorders, for instance, can be critical in profiling serial killers or sex offenders.

- **Criminological Theories**: Criminological theories help in understanding the motivations behind crimes and the social contexts that may contribute to criminal behavior.

Challenges and Criticisms of Criminal Profiling

- **Subjectivity**: One criticism of profiling is its inherent subjectivity. The interpretation of crime scene data can vary, leading to different profiles.

- **Accuracy and Reliability**: The accuracy of profiles and their success rate in leading to the apprehension of offenders has been a subject of debate among professionals.

- **Ethical Considerations**: Profiling must be conducted ethically, avoiding biases based on race, ethnicity, or socioeconomic status.

Applications of Criminal Profiling

- **Law Enforcement**: Profiling assists law enforcement agencies in narrowing down suspect lists and focusing investigative resources effectively.

- **Legal Proceedings**: Sometimes, criminal profiles are used in court to support cases against suspects.

- **Research and Training**: Profiling contributes to the broader understanding of criminal behavior and is used for training law enforcement and criminal justice professionals.

Techniques in Understanding Criminal Behavior

Behavioral analysis in criminal psychology is a method used to understand and interpret the behavior of criminals. It involves examining various aspects of a criminal's actions and patterns to gain insights into their motives, intentions, and characteristics. Behavioral analysis is grounded in the concept that behavior, especially criminal behavior, is not random but purposeful and reflective of an individual's personality and psychological state. It uses principles from various psychological disciplines, including cognitive psychology, social psychology, and psychopathology.

Key Techniques in Behavioral Analysis

- **Crime Scene Analysis**: The analysis of a crime scene provides critical insights into a criminal's behavior. This includes examining the location, mode of operation, and the nature of the interaction with the victim. Organized versus disorganized crime scenes can suggest different personality types and levels of planning.

- **Victimology**: Understanding the victims of a crime is crucial. This involves studying their background, lifestyle, and the nature of their interaction with the offender. Victimology can reveal why certain individuals were targeted and the offender's possible motivations.

- **Pattern Recognition and Linkage Analysis**: This involves identifying patterns in crimes, which can indicate a single offender's involvement in multiple crimes. Linkage analysis helps in connecting different crimes based on method, style, and the offender's signature.

- **Interview and Interrogation Techniques**: Skillful interviewing and interrogation are vital in behavioral analysis. This includes analyzing verbal and nonverbal cues, understanding the psychology of lying, and using techniques to elicit truthful responses.

- **Offender Typologies**: Developing typologies or classifications of offenders based on their behaviors, motives, and characteristics helps in understanding and predicting criminal behavior. This can be particularly useful in serial crime cases.

- **Geographical Profiling**: This technique examines the locations of a series of crimes to determine the most probable area of an offender's residence or base of operations. It is based on the principle that criminals often commit crimes within a comfort zone near their familiar areas.

- **Digital Behavior Analysis**: In the case of cybercrime, analyzing digital behaviors, such as online communication patterns and digital footprints, is essential. This includes understanding how criminals use technology and the internet to commit crimes.

Challenges in Behavioral Analysis

- **Subjectivity and Bias**: One of the challenges in behavioral analysis is the potential for subjectivity and bias. It requires analysts to be meticulous in their approach and to base their conclusions on evidence rather than personal assumptions.

- **Complexity of Human Behavior**: Human behavior, particularly in the context of crime, is complex and influenced by various factors. Behavioral analysts must consider a wide range of potential influences, including mental health issues, environmental factors, and past experiences.

- **Evolving Nature of Crime**: As criminal methods evolve, especially with advancements in technology, behavioral analysts must continuously update their knowledge and adapt their techniques.

Behavioral analysis aids in profiling offenders, guiding investigative strategies, and identifying potential future risks. It also contributes to the development of intervention programs and informs decisions in the judicial process.

Geographical Profiling

Geographical profiling is a strategic tool in criminal psychology, used to analyze locations connected to a series of crimes to determine the most probable area where an offender might live or operate. This method combines principles of environmental criminology, geography, and psychology, offering insights into the spatial behavior of criminals.

Geographical profiling is based on the premise that the locations of crimes are not random but are significant in understanding an offender's behavior. Offenders typically commit crimes within a comfort zone, an area they know well and feel secure in. By analyzing crime locations, profilers can infer patterns and predict the offender's likely base of operations.

The Process of Geographical Profiling

- **Data Collection and Mapping**: The first step involves collecting data on the locations of the connected crimes. Modern geographic information systems (GIS) are often used to map these locations, providing a visual representation of the crime sites.

- **Crime Location Analysis**: Analysts study the distribution and proximity of the crime locations. Factors like the type of location, accessibility, escape routes, and geographic features are considered.

- **Behavioral Inference**: Based on the pattern of the locations, profilers draw inferences about the offender's behavior. This includes movement patterns, transportation methods, and lifestyle habits.

- **Offender's Anchor Points**: Profilers identify possible 'anchor points' - locations significant to the offender, such as their home, workplace, or social hangouts. The majority of criminals operate within a comfort zone near these anchor points.

- **Creation of the Geographical Profile**: The analysis leads to the creation of a geographical profile, which highlights areas where the offender is likely to be found. It often includes a 'hot zone' which has a higher probability of containing the offender's base.

Applications of Geographical Profiling

- **Serial Crimes**: Geographical profiling is particularly useful in cases of serial crimes, such as serial murders, rapes, or arsons. It helps in understanding the spatial behavior of the offender across multiple incidents.

- **Resource Allocation**: Law enforcement agencies use geographical profiles to allocate resources more effectively, focusing investigative efforts in areas with a higher probability of finding the offender.

- **Predicting Future Crimes**: This technique can also be used to predict potential future crime sites based on the offender's known pattern, assisting in prevention and surveillance efforts.

Psychological Aspects in Geographical Profiling

- **Territoriality**: The concept of territoriality is central in geographical profiling. Criminals often display territorial behavior, committing crimes within areas they are familiar with and comfortable in.

- **Routine Activity Theory**: This theory suggests that crimes occur when a potential offender's routine intersects with a suitable target in the absence of capable guardians. Analyzing the offender's routine can reveal patterns in their criminal activity.

- **Environmental Criminology**: Geographical profiling incorporates principles of environmental criminology, which studies how the physical environment influences criminal behavior.

Challenges and Limitations

- **Accuracy**: While geographical profiling can be highly valuable, its accuracy depends on the quality and quantity of crime location data available.

- **Dynamic Nature of Human Behavior**: Offenders may change their behavior or patterns over time, impacting the reliability of the geographical profile.

- **Integration with Other Profiling Methods**: For the best results, geographical profiling should be integrated with other criminal profiling methods for a comprehensive understanding of the offender.

Profiling in the Digital Age

Cyber profiling represents a significant evolution in the field of criminal psychology, adapting traditional profiling techniques to the digital age. As criminal activities increasingly move into the online realm, understanding the psychological and behavioral patterns of cybercriminals has become essential.

Cyber profiling is based on the premise that, just as in the physical world, criminal behavior online is influenced by an individual's personality, motivations, and psychological traits. By examining how these criminals behave in the digital environment, profilers can infer their characteristics, motivations, and potential future actions.

Techniques in Cyber Profiling

- **Analysis of Digital Footprints**: Cyber profilers examine the digital footprints left by individuals on websites, social media platforms, and various online forums. This includes scrutinizing communication patterns, posting habits, and interaction styles.

- **Behavioral Patterns in Cybercrimes**: Profilers study the methods and techniques used in cybercrimes, looking for patterns that might link different offenses and point to specific offender profiles. This can include the analysis of malware, phishing tactics, or the structure of fraudulent schemes.

- **Psycholinguistic Analysis**: The way language is used in online communications can provide insights into a cybercriminal's personality and background. This includes examining word choice, grammar, and spelling, which can indicate education level, cultural background, or even geographical location.

- **Online Interactions and Social Networks**: Analyzing an individual's interactions and networks online can reveal their social habits, preferences, and potentially radical or deviant affiliations. This is particularly relevant in cases of online radicalization or cyberbullying.

- **Technological Proficiency**: The level of technical skill displayed in committing cybercrimes can also help in profiling. Highly sophisticated attacks may point to a more educated and experienced individual or group, whereas less sophisticated crimes might indicate opportunistic or novice offenders.

Applications of Cyber Profiling

- **Law Enforcement and Investigations**: Cyber profiling is increasingly used by law enforcement agencies to track and apprehend cybercriminals. By understanding the behavioral patterns unique to certain types of cybercrimes, investigators can narrow down suspects and predict potential targets.

- **Prevention of Cybercrimes**: Profiling potential cybercriminals can aid in the development of preventative strategies, including cybersecurity measures tailored to specific types of attacks.

- **Corporate Security**: Businesses and organizations use cyber profiling to protect against insider threats and external cyber attacks. Understanding the profile of potential cyber attackers can help in implementing effective security protocols.

Challenges in Cyber Profiling

- **Anonymity and Deception**: The anonymous nature of the internet poses a significant challenge in cyber profiling. Offenders may use various methods to conceal their identity, making it difficult to gather accurate data for profiling.

- **Evolving Technology**: Rapid technological advancements mean that cyber profilers must continuously update their knowledge and adapt their techniques to new digital environments and emerging cyber threats.

- **Ethical and Legal Considerations**: Cyber profiling must navigate the complex terrain of online privacy, data protection laws, and ethical considerations related to surveillance and data collection.

How to Recognize a Criminal in Daily Life

The endeavor to identify a criminal in the midst of everyday life is a complex and nuanced task. Recognizing that not all criminals manifest easily identifiable traits, and conversely, not all individuals displaying such traits are criminals, is crucial. The focus here is on enhancing awareness rather than fostering suspicion.

Antisocial Behavior: A prominent indicator is a pattern of antisocial behavior, which includes a disregard for social norms, laws, and the rights of others. This can manifest as deceitfulness, impulsivity, irritability, and aggressiveness. In everyday interactions, this might be evident in consistent rule-breaking, a tendency to lie or manipulate, and unprovoked aggression.

Manipulative Tendencies: Many criminals are adept at manipulation, using charm and charisma to deceive and exploit others. Be wary of individuals who consistently employ flattery or persuasion to achieve their ends, particularly if their actions reveal a disregard for others' well-being.

Inconsistent Lifestyle: Criminals may lead lifestyles marked by inconsistency and instability. This could manifest as frequent job changes, lack of long-term goals, or an inability to maintain steady relationships. While these traits can be indicative of other issues, in conjunction with other signs, they may suggest criminal tendencies.

History of Trouble: A past marked by repeated trouble with law enforcement or involvement in questionable activities can be a red flag. However, it is essential to differentiate between someone who has made mistakes and reformed from those who persist in criminal behavior.

Thrill-Seeking Behavior: An inclination towards risky, thrill-seeking behavior, often without regard for safety or consequences, can be a sign. This includes a penchant for dangerous activities, reckless driving, or substance abuse.

Criminals are not created in a vacuum. Often, environmental and social factors play a significant role in the development of criminal behavior. These include a troubled childhood, exposure to violence or crime at a young age, lack of positive role models, or socio-economic hardships. Understanding these factors is vital in recognizing potential criminal tendencies and offering appropriate support or intervention.

While not a scientific tool, intuition or gut feeling can sometimes alert us to something amiss in someone's behavior or demeanor. Trusting your instincts while remaining objective can be a valuable part of recognizing potential criminal behavior.

Chapter Seven: Interrogation and Lie Detection

Lie Detection Methods

Over the years, various methods have been developed and used to detect lies. The polygraph is perhaps the most well-known of these methods, but advancements in technology and psychology have led to the exploration of additional techniques.

The Polygraph Test

The polygraph, commonly known as the lie detector, measures and records physiological indices such as blood pressure, pulse, respiration, and skin conductivity while the subject answers a series of questions. The underlying principle is that deceptive answers will produce physiological responses that can be differentiated from those associated with non-deceptive answers.

- **Mechanics of the Polygraph**: The polygraph test typically involves a pre-test interview, the polygraph examination itself, and a post-test analysis. The pre-test phase includes formulating control and relevant questions and familiarizing the subject with the test process.

- **Interpretation of Results**: The polygraph examiner analyzes the recorded physiological responses to the questions. Significant reactions to relevant questions, as compared to control questions, may suggest deception.

- **Limitations and Controversies**: The accuracy of polygraph testing has been a subject of debate. Factors like nervousness, fear, or belief in the accuracy of the polygraph can influence the results. Additionally, it is possible for individuals to train themselves to control their physiological responses, potentially leading to false negatives.

Behavioral Analysis

Behavioral analysis involves observing and interpreting a person's behavior during an interview or interrogation to detect deception. This includes analyzing verbal cues, body language, and facial expressions.

- **Microexpressions**: These are involuntary facial expressions that occur within a fraction of a second. They can be indicative of a person's true emotions and are often analyzed in lie detection.

- **Verbal Cues**: Inconsistencies in a story, evasive answers, or changes in speech patterns can be indicators of deception.

- **Nonverbal Cues**: Body language such as avoidance of eye contact, fidgeting, or other nervous behaviors can sometimes suggest that a person is being deceptive.

Neuroscientific Approaches

Advancements in neuroscience have led to the development of methods that assess brain activity for lie detection.

- **Functional Magnetic Resonance Imaging (fMRI)**: fMRI is used to measure and map brain activity. The idea is that lying requires more cognitive effort than telling the truth, and this increased effort can be detected as changes in brain activity.

- **Event-Related Potential (ERP)**: This technique measures the brain's electrical activity in response to stimuli. Certain types of ERPs are believed to be associated with deceptive behaviors.

- **Limitations**: Neuroscientific methods are still in the experimental stages for lie detection. Issues such as high costs, the need for controlled environments, and ethical concerns about brain privacy limit their widespread use.

Voice Stress Analysis

Voice stress analysis (VSA) is another technique employed to detect lies. It works on the premise that psychological stress caused by lying will affect the properties of a person's voice.

- **Methodology**: VSA involves the analysis of micro-tremors in the voice. These tremors are thought to decrease during stress, including the stress of deception.

- **Effectiveness and Critique**: Like the polygraph, the reliability of VSA is debated. Factors unrelated to deception, such as anxiety or excitement, can affect voice tremors, leading to potential inaccuracies.

How to Recognize Lies in Daily Life

Lying is a behavior ingrained in human nature, used for various reasons ranging from self-preservation to manipulation. Recognizing lies is not merely about spotting a false statement; it's about understanding the context, the speaker's normal behavior, and the subtle cues that signal dishonesty.

Inconsistencies in Storytelling

One of the most significant indicators of lying is inconsistency in storytelling. When a person fabricates a story, maintaining coherence and remembering each fabricated detail becomes a challenging task. Over time, these stories often evolve or contradict previously stated facts. This inconsistency can manifest in several ways:

- **Altering Details**: A liar might change key details of their story upon retelling. This could be minor elements like times and places or significant aspects of the event.

- **Contradictory Information**: In their attempt to seem credible, liars often introduce new elements that contradict their initial statements. These contradictions are usually subtle but become more apparent under careful scrutiny.

- **Complex vs. Simplified Narratives**: Liars may either overly complicate a story to distract and confuse the listener or oversimplify to avoid getting caught in a lie. Both strategies create an unnatural narrative flow that can be a red flag.

Changes in Speech Patterns

Lies require cognitive effort, often leading to noticeable changes in speech patterns. These changes can include:

- **Speech Hesitations and Pauses**: When crafting a lie, individuals might pause more often as they think about what to say next. These pauses are usually filled with filler words like "um" and "uh."

- **Altered Speech Pace**: A liar might speed up their speech unconsciously, trying to get through the lie quickly. Conversely, some slow down, carefully choosing their words to avoid slipping up.

- **Voice Modulation**: Changes in pitch, tone, or volume can also indicate lying. A higher pitch may indicate stress or nervousness, while a suddenly softer tone might be an attempt to appear sincere or convincing.

Behavioral Cues and Body Language

Non-verbal cues are often more telling than verbal ones, as they are harder to control:

- **Facial Expressions**: Micro-expressions, fleeting involuntary facial expressions, can betray a person's true emotions, even if they are trying to conceal them.

For instance, a flash of fear or guilt on someone's face when they deny wrongdoing.

- **Body Language Discrepancies**: Incongruence between what a person is saying and their body language is a key indicator of lying. For example, someone claiming happiness while their body language shows tension or closed-off gestures.

- **Avoidance Behaviors**: Avoiding eye contact, frequent touching of the face, or shifting posture can suggest discomfort, which may be related to lying. However, it's important to note that such behaviors can also stem from anxiety or shyness.

The Psychological Manipulations

In the realm of criminal psychology, the study of how criminals manipulate their victims and environment is a subject of profound importance.

Types of Psychological Manipulation

- **Grooming**: Often seen in cases of sexual abuse or exploitation, grooming involves building a trusting relationship with a potential victim. Offenders may shower the victim with attention, gifts, or affection to lower their defenses and gain control over them. This tactic is particularly insidious as it can lead the victim to feel complicit in the criminal activity.

- **Gaslighting**: Gaslighting is a manipulative technique where the offender causes a victim to doubt their own memories or perceptions. It's a form of psychological control that can lead to the victim questioning their sanity. In domestic abuse cases, for instance, abusers may insist that events did not happen as the victim remembers them, thereby undermining the victim's sense of reality.

- **Coercion and Threats**: Coercion involves forcing someone to do something against their will by using threats or intimidation. This can range from overt threats of physical harm to more subtle forms of coercion, such as blackmail or the threat of revealing sensitive information.

- **Exploitation of Power Dynamics**: Many criminals exploit power imbalances in their relationships with victims. This can be seen in workplace harassment, where a superior abuses their position, or in cases where adults exploit children or vulnerable individuals.

- **Isolation**: Isolating the victim from friends, family, and support systems is a common tactic used by abusers. This isolation makes the victim more dependent on the offender, thereby increasing the offender's control.

- **Projection and Blaming**: Offenders often project their own faults onto their victims or blame their victims for their actions. This not only serves to justify the offender's behavior but also aims to shift responsibility onto the victim.

Psychological Underpinnings

- **Need for Power and Control**: Many manipulative behaviors stem from a perpetrator's need for power and control over others. This is often rooted in deep-seated insecurities and a desire to dominate.

- **Lack of Empathy**: A key characteristic of many offenders is a lack of empathy. Their inability to recognize or care about the impact of their actions on others allows them to manipulate without remorse.

- **Antisocial Personality Traits**: Individuals with antisocial personality disorder or other related personality disorders are more likely to engage in manipulative behavior. They often exhibit a disregard for social norms and the rights of others.

- **Learned Behavior**: In some cases, manipulative behavior is learned. Offenders may have been exposed to manipulation in their own upbringing or have learned that such tactics are effective in getting what they want.

The impact of criminal manipulation on victims can be devastating. It can lead to psychological trauma, a loss of trust, diminished self-esteem, and mental health issues such as anxiety, depression, and PTSD. Recovery from such manipulation often requires long-term psychological support.

How to Recognize a Manipulator

Notice: It's crucial to remember that while certain behaviors may suggest manipulative tendencies, they do not conclusively define someone as a manipulator.

Key Characteristics of Manipulators

Charm and Charisma: Manipulators often possess an engaging and captivating personality. They are adept at using charm as a tool to gain trust and influence. This charm can manifest as flattery, attention, and seemingly genuine interest in others' lives. However, it's important to discern genuine charisma from manipulative charm, which is usually self-serving and lacks depth.

- **Intensity of Interaction**: In the early stages of interaction, a manipulator may exhibit intense and overwhelming charm. They might shower you with compliments, attention, and what appears to be affection, to quickly establish a connection.

- **Shift in Behavior**: Observe the consistency of their charm. Manipulators often shift from being exceptionally charming to cold and indifferent, especially when they no longer need something from the person.

Emotional Exploitation: Manipulators are skilled in exploiting others' emotions to their advantage. They may use guilt, sympathy, or fear as tools to control their targets. This exploitation often involves playing the victim, exaggerating problems, or fabricating crises to elicit sympathy and manipulate others into compliance.

- **Creating Obligations**: A manipulator may remind you of the favors they've done or the sacrifices they've made, creating a sense of obligation. This is often coupled with guilt-tripping, making the person feel they owe something in return.

- **Emotional Blackmail**: They may use sensitive information or shared secrets as leverage, employing emotional blackmail to get what they want.

Gaslighting and Reality Distortion: Gaslighting is a common manipulative technique where the manipulator causes someone to question their own reality, memory, or perceptions. This method is insidious and can be incredibly damaging to the victim's sense of self and reality.

- **Denial of Facts**: Even when presented with evidence, a manipulator might deny the facts or their actions, insisting that the other person is misremembering or overreacting.

- **Undermining Confidence**: They often undermine the other person's confidence in their judgment, subtly suggesting that they are too sensitive, paranoid, or mentally unstable.

Isolation and Control: Manipulators seek to isolate their targets from their support systems, such as friends and family, to gain more control. This isolation is often gradual and subtle.

- **Criticism of Loved Ones**: They might start by subtly criticizing your close relationships, planting seeds of doubt about the intentions of your friends or family members.

- **Restricting Social Interaction**: Over time, they may escalate to more overt attempts to limit your social interactions, either through direct requests or by creating situations that make it difficult for you to maintain other relationships.

Foundations of Interrogation Psychology

Interrogation techniques are grounded in understanding the cognitive and emotional processes of individuals. This includes recognizing how memory works, how stress impacts cognition and behavior, and how rapport can be built and utilized. A successful interrogation balances the need to gather accurate information with the rights and well-being of the individual being interrogated.

Key Techniques and Strategies in Interrogation

- Rapport Building: Establishing rapport is a fundamental strategy. It involves creating a connection and a sense of trust with the person being interrogated. This can make them more comfortable and willing to share information. Techniques include showing empathy, active listening, and respecting their dignity.

- Cognitive Interviewing: This technique is designed to enhance memory retrieval. It involves asking open-ended questions, allowing the person to recount events in their own words, and using various prompts to help jog their memory without leading them to specific conclusions.

- Reid Technique: A controversial method that involves a more accusatory approach. It starts with an interview to assess the suspect's credibility and then moves to a nine-step interrogation process designed to elicit a confession. This technique is criticized for its potential to lead to false confessions.

- The PEACE Model: An alternative to the Reid technique, the PEACE model (Preparation and Planning, Engage and Explain, Account, Closure, and Evaluate) focuses on gathering accurate information rather than eliciting a confession. It emphasizes ethical interrogation, rapport building, and allowing the interviewee to give their account without interruption or coercion.

- Controlled Questioning: This involves carefully structuring questions to control the flow of the interrogation. Closed and open-ended questions are used strategically to confirm details, clarify information, and explore discrepancies in the narrative.

- Behavioral Analysis: This includes analyzing verbal and non-verbal cues to assess truthfulness and stress. Indicators such as changes in speech patterns, body language, and eye movements can provide clues about the individual's state of mind and honesty.

Challenges and Ethical Considerations

- Avoiding Coercion: It's crucial to avoid any form of coercion or intimidation, as these can lead to false confessions or unreliable information. Interrogators must be mindful of the power dynamics at play.

- Memory and Suggestibility: Human memory is fallible and suggestible. Interrogators must be careful not to inadvertently implant ideas or memories through leading questions or assumptions.

- Cultural Sensitivity: Understanding and respecting cultural differences is essential, as these can influence communication styles, perceptions of authority, and responses to interrogation techniques.

- Legal and Ethical Boundaries: Interrogations should always operate within the boundaries of the law and ethical guidelines. This includes respecting the rights of the individual and ensuring that any information or confession is obtained legally and ethically.

The Psychology of Confession: Why Criminals Confess

Confessions are a crucial element in the criminal justice system, often serving as compelling evidence in legal proceedings. However, the reasons why individuals admit to criminal behavior can vary widely, encompassing a complex interplay of psychological factors, situational influences, and interrogation techniques.

Psychological Drivers of Confessions

- **Guilt and Remorse**: One of the primary reasons for confessions is a sense of guilt or remorse. Some individuals may confess because they feel morally compelled to atone for their actions. The psychological burden of guilt can be overwhelming, prompting a need for relief which confession provides.

- **Seeking Closure**: For some offenders, confessing is a means to seek closure. They may wish to end the stress of hiding their actions or resolve inner conflict, and confession offers a way to confront and deal with their deeds.

- **Fear of Detection**: The fear of eventual detection, especially in high-profile or extensively investigated cases, can lead to confessions. Individuals might believe that confessing will afford them more lenient treatment compared to being caught later.

- **Desire for Notoriety**: In certain cases, particularly with serial crimes, the offender may crave recognition for their actions. Confessing can be a way to gain notoriety and attention.

- **Protecting Others**: Some confessions arise from a desire to protect someone else. This could be a loved one whom the offender wishes to shield from suspicion or legal consequences.

False Confessions: Causes and Consequences

False confessions, where an individual admits to a crime they did not commit, represent a critical issue in criminal psychology and the justice system.

Causes of False Confessions

- **Coercive Interrogation Techniques**: High-pressure interrogation methods can lead to false confessions. Techniques like prolonged questioning, lack of sleep, threats, and promises of leniency can make individuals feel compelled to confess, regardless of their guilt.

- **Vulnerability of the Interrogated**: Certain groups, such as juveniles, individuals with cognitive impairments, or those with mental health issues, are more susceptible to making false confessions. They may have a limited understanding of their rights or the implications of confessing.

- **Misunderstanding or Misinterpretation of the Situation**: A suspect might misunderstand the nature of the evidence against them, believing that a confession is their only option, even if they are innocent.

- **Fear of Violence or Retribution**: In some cases, suspects confess to protect themselves or their loved ones from perceived threats of violence or retribution.

- **Desire to End the Interrogation**: The stress and discomfort of a prolonged interrogation can lead individuals to confess simply to end the experience, especially if they believe they can later prove their innocence.

- **Internalized False Confessions**: In some instances, especially after intense or manipulative interrogations, suspects may come to believe they committed the crime, despite having no memory of it. This internalization can be influenced by suggestibility, fatigue, and psychological manipulation.

Consequences of False Confessions

- **Wrongful Convictions**: One of the most serious consequences of false confessions is the wrongful conviction of innocent individuals. This not only destroys the lives of these individuals and their families but also undermines public trust in the justice system.

- **Impact on the Actual Investigation**: False confessions can lead law enforcement away from the real perpetrator, allowing them to remain at large and potentially commit more crimes.

- **Psychological Impact on the Confessor**: Individuals who falsely confess can suffer significant psychological trauma, including feelings of guilt, shame, and anxiety. The stigma and legal ramifications of a false confession can have long-term effects on mental health and social standing.

- **Legal and Social Ramifications**: Beyond imprisonment, a false confession can lead to social ostracism, loss of employment, and financial burdens related to legal fees and restitution.

Preventing False Confessions

- **Reformed Interrogation Techniques**: Implementing ethical interrogation practices that avoid coercion and respect the rights of suspects is essential in preventing false confessions.

- **Recording Interrogations**: Recording interrogations in their entirety provides an accurate record of the interaction between law enforcement and the suspect, helping to ensure fair treatment.

- **Training for Law Enforcement**: Providing comprehensive training to law enforcement officials on the risks of false confessions and how to conduct ethical interrogations is crucial.

- **Legal Safeguards**: Ensuring that suspects have access to legal counsel and are fully informed of their rights can help prevent false confessions.

- **Public Awareness and Education**: Educating the public, including vulnerable groups, about their rights during police interrogations can empower individuals to resist coercive tactics.

Chapter Eight: Mental Illness and Criminal Behavior

Mental illness refers to a wide range of mental health conditions that affect mood, thinking, and behavior. These conditions include disorders such as depression, anxiety disorders, schizophrenia, and bipolar disorder. Mental illnesses can significantly impair an individual's ability to think, feel, and relate to others, impacting daily functioning and quality of life.

Criminality, on the other hand, involves engaging in actions that violate societal laws and norms. It encompasses a broad spectrum of behaviors, from minor infractions to serious crimes. Criminal behavior is influenced by a variety of factors, including environment, upbringing, social and economic circumstances, and individual choice.

Key Distinctions Between Mental Illness and Criminality

- **Nature of the Behavior**: Mental illness is characterized by symptoms and behaviors that are typically involuntary and stem from underlying mental health conditions. Criminal behavior is characterized by actions that violate the law, which are typically viewed as a choice or decision made by the individual.

- **Motivation and Intent**: In mental illness, behaviors may be driven by symptoms such as delusions, hallucinations, or impaired judgment. In criminality, behaviors are often motivated by factors such as gain, revenge, or desire.

- **Legal Responsibility and Competency**: The legal system differentiates between individuals with mental illness and those engaging in criminal behavior in terms of responsibility and competency. An individual with a severe mental illness may be deemed not criminally responsible or incompetent to stand trial if their condition significantly impairs their ability to understand or control their actions.

- **Assessment and Diagnosis**: Mental illnesses are diagnosed based on criteria in diagnostic manuals like the DSM-5 (Diagnostic and Statistical Manual of Mental Disorders). Criminal behavior is assessed based on legal definitions and evidence of law-breaking actions.

- **Treatment vs. Punishment**: The approach to mental illness is primarily treatment-oriented, focusing on managing symptoms and improving quality of life. The approach to criminality, especially when it is not related to mental illness, is more punitive, focusing on retribution, deterrence, and rehabilitation.

There are cases where mental illness and criminality intersect. For example, an individual with a severe mental illness might engage in criminal behavior as a result of their condition. In such cases, it is crucial to carefully assess the role of the mental illness in the behavior to determine the most appropriate response.

Differentiating between mental illness and criminality can be challenging, particularly in cases where symptoms of a mental disorder might influence or exacerbate criminal behavior. Mental health professionals and legal experts often need to work together to assess each case.

When dealing with individuals with mental illness who have committed crimes, there is a need for ethical consideration to ensure that they receive appropriate treatment and that their rights are respected. The justice system must balance public safety with the need to provide care for the mentally ill.

Specific Mental Disorders and Crime

While the majority of individuals with mental disorders do not engage in criminal activities, there are certain conditions where a higher incidence of criminal behavior has been observed.

Schizophrenia and Psychotic Disorders

- **Nature of the Disorder**: Schizophrenia and related psychotic disorders are characterized by delusions, hallucinations, disorganized thinking, and impaired reality testing.

- **Connection to Crime**: While the majority of individuals with schizophrenia are not violent, a small subset may engage in criminal behavior, often influenced by psychotic symptoms such as delusions or command hallucinations. These individuals might misconstrue reality in a way that leads to fear or perceived threats, resulting in defensive aggression.

- **Risk Factors**: The risk of criminal behavior increases if the disorder is untreated or combined with substance abuse. Lack of insight into their illness can also increase the risk.

Antisocial Personality Disorder (ASPD)

- **Nature of the Disorders**: ASPD is characterized by a pervasive pattern of disregard for and violation of the rights of others. Psychopathy, although not a formal diagnosis in many diagnostic manuals, is characterized by a lack of empathy, superficial charm, manipulativeness, and often, criminal behavior.

- **Connection to Crime**: Individuals with ASPD or psychopathic traits are more likely to engage in criminal behavior, including violent crimes. Their lack of empathy, disregard for societal norms, and impulsivity contribute to this propensity.

- **Considerations**: Not all individuals with ASPD or psychopathic traits commit crimes, and not all criminals meet the criteria for these disorders. However, the prevalence of ASPD and psychopathy is significantly higher in prison populations than in the general public.

Depression and Bipolar Disorder

- **Nature of the Disorders**: Depression is characterized by persistent sadness and loss of interest. Bipolar disorder involves alternating periods of depression and mania.

- **Connection to Crime**: The relationship between mood disorders and crime is less direct. In some cases, depressive disorders can lead to substance abuse, which may increase the risk of criminal behavior. In the case of bipolar disorder, impulsive and risky behaviors during manic phases can lead to criminal activities.

- **Risk Factors**: Substance abuse and a lack of treatment or non-compliance with treatment can increase the risk of criminal behavior in individuals with mood disorders.

Substance Use Disorders

- **Nature of the Disorder**: Substance use disorders involve the problematic use of substances like alcohol, drugs, and prescription medications.

- **Connection to Crime**: Substance use disorders are strongly linked to criminal behavior, including drug-related crimes, theft, and offenses committed under the influence.

- **Considerations**: The criminal behavior is often directly related to the substance abuse (e.g., possession, distribution) or indirectly related (e.g., committing a crime to obtain money for substances).

ADHD and Criminal Behavior

- **Nature of the Disorder**: Attention-Deficit/Hyperactivity Disorder (ADHD) is characterized by inattention, hyperactivity, and impulsivity.

- **Connection to Crime**: Individuals with ADHD may be at a higher risk for engaging in criminal behavior, largely due to impulsivity and poor decision-making.

- **Risk Factors**: Co-occurring conditions such as conduct disorder or substance abuse can increase the risk of criminal behavior in individuals with ADHD.

Insanity Defense and Mental Health Laws

The legal implications of mental health in criminal cases revolve around the assessment of a defendant's mental state at the time of the crime and their ability to understand and participate in legal proceedings.

The insanity defense is a legal concept that allows a defendant to argue that they should not be held criminally responsible for their actions due to a severe mental illness or defect.

- **Legal Standards for Insanity**: Various standards are used to determine insanity, including the M'Naghten Rule (lack of understanding of right and wrong), the Irresistible Impulse Test (inability to control actions), and the Model Penal Code (lack of substantial capacity to appreciate the criminality of conduct or conform conduct to the law).

- **Application and Evaluation**: The insanity defense is applied in cases where there is significant evidence that the defendant was suffering from a severe mental illness at the time of the crime. Psychiatric evaluations and expert testimony are crucial in establishing the defendant's mental state.

- **Outcomes**: If a defendant is found not guilty by reason of insanity, they are typically committed to a psychiatric facility for treatment rather than being sent to prison. The length of commitment can vary and is often contingent on the individual's response to treatment and risk assessment.

Competency to Stand Trial

Determining a defendant's competency to stand trial is another critical aspect of mental health in the legal system. Competency refers to the defendant's ability to understand the charges against them and participate in their defense.

- **Evaluation of Competency**: This involves assessing whether the defendant understands the legal proceedings and can effectively communicate with their attorney. Mental health professionals play a key role in this evaluation.

- **Consequences of Incompetence**: If a defendant is deemed incompetent, legal proceedings are typically halted. The individual may be placed in a treatment facility until they are deemed competent to stand trial.

Mental Health Laws and Sentencing

Mental health considerations also play a role in sentencing decisions.

- **Mitigating Factors**: Mental illness can be considered a mitigating factor in sentencing, potentially leading to reduced sentences or alternative forms of punishment, such as mandated treatment.

- **Mandatory Treatment Orders**: In some cases, the court may order mandatory mental health treatment as part of a sentence, either in lieu of incarceration or in addition to it.

Ethical and Legal Challenges

- **Balancing Public Safety and Individual Rights**: One of the primary challenges is balancing the rights of individuals with mental illness against the need to protect public safety.

- **Stigma and Misconceptions**: The insanity defense is often misunderstood and stigmatized, leading to misconceptions about its use and implications.

- **Resource Limitations**: The availability of mental health resources, including treatment facilities and expert evaluators, can be limited, impacting the justice system's ability to effectively address mental health issues.

Balancing Rehabilitation and Justice

One of the most significant debates revolves around the balance between treatment and punishment. This debate focuses on how to address criminal behavior in a way that serves the interests of justice, protects society, and supports the rehabilitation of offenders. The integration of these approaches poses complex challenges and requires a nuanced understanding of criminal behavior, its causes, and the most effective ways to address it.

Behind Punishment and Rehabilitation

- **Punishment**: Traditionally, the criminal justice system has emphasized punishment. Punishment is based on the principles of retribution, deterrence, and incapacitation. It focuses on penalizing the offender for the wrongs committed, deterring others from committing similar crimes, and protecting society by removing dangerous individuals.

- **Rehabilitation**: Rehabilitation, on the other hand, focuses on treating and educating offenders to prevent future criminal behavior. It involves understanding the underlying factors that led to the crime, such as substance abuse, mental health issues, or socio-economic circumstances, and addressing these issues through various treatment programs.

Balancing the Two Approaches

- **Nature of the Crime**: The balance between treatment and punishment often depends on the nature and severity of the crime. Violent and serious crimes may lean more towards punishment, while crimes driven by underlying issues like addiction or mental health problems may be more amenable to rehabilitation.

- **Risk Assessment**: Assessing the risk an offender poses to society is crucial. High-risk individuals may require a combination of incarceration (punishment) and treatment to reduce the risk of reoffending.

- **Individual Assessment**: Tailoring the approach to the individual is important. This involves evaluating the offender's background, psychological state, and the factors that contributed to the criminal behavior.

- **Effectiveness of Rehabilitation Programs**: The success of rehabilitation depends on the availability and effectiveness of treatment programs. These programs can include therapy, educational and vocational training, and support in reintegrating into society.

Ethical and Legal Considerations

- **Justice for Victims**: Balancing treatment and punishment must also consider the needs and rights of victims. The justice system needs to ensure that victims feel that justice has been served.

- **Rights of Offenders**: Offenders have the right to fair and humane treatment. This includes access to effective rehabilitation programs and being free from cruel or excessive punishment.

- **Public Safety**: The primary goal of the criminal justice system is to protect public safety. Balancing treatment and punishment should not compromise this objective.

Challenges in Implementing a Balanced Approach

- **Resource Limitations**: Effective rehabilitation programs require significant resources, including trained professionals, facilities, and ongoing support systems.

- **Public Perception**: There is often public skepticism about the effectiveness of rehabilitation, particularly for serious crimes. Balancing public opinion with evidence-based approaches to criminal behavior is a challenge.

- **Recidivism**: One of the measures of success for rehabilitation is the rate of recidivism. Ensuring that offenders do not re-offend is crucial for validating the effectiveness of rehabilitation programs.

- **Integrating Rehabilitation into the Justice System**: Seamlessly integrating treatment programs into the criminal justice system requires coordination between various agencies, including law enforcement, judicial systems, mental health services, and social services.

Cases: Notable Instances Where Mental Illness Played a Role

Here, we explore several key instances where mental illness played a critical role in criminal cases.

John Hinckley Jr. and the Attempted Assassination of President Reagan

In 1981, John Hinckley Jr. attempted to assassinate U.S. President Ronald Reagan. The case became a landmark in the discussion of mental illness and crime. Hinckley was found not guilty by reason of insanity, leading to widespread public debate and subsequent reforms in the use of the insanity defense.

Hinckley was diagnosed with schizophrenia and narcissistic personality disorder. His actions were reportedly driven by an obsession with actress Jodie Foster, rooted in delusional thinking.

The verdict brought significant attention to the criteria used to assess legal insanity and prompted changes in laws governing the insanity defense across several states.

Andrea Yates and Filicide

Andrea Yates, who drowned her five children in 2001, is another tragic instance of mental illness intersecting with criminal behavior. Yates' case highlighted issues related to postpartum psychosis and the legal system's handling of mental illness.

Yates suffered from severe postpartum depression and psychosis. She experienced delusions that she was saving her children from damnation.

Initially convicted of capital murder, Yates was later found not guilty by reason of insanity in a retrial. Her case underscored the need for awareness and treatment of postpartum mental health issues.

The Unabomber, Ted Kaczynski

Ted Kaczynski, known as the Unabomber, carried out a series of bombings over nearly two decades, motivated by an anti-technology philosophy. His case is an intersection of extreme ideological beliefs and potential mental health issues.

Kaczynski exhibited signs of paranoia and social withdrawal. While he was competent to stand trial, discussions about his mental health, including possible schizophrenia, were central to understanding his motives.

Kaczynski pled guilty to avoid the death penalty and was sentenced to life imprisonment without the possibility of parole.

The Virginia Tech Shooting and Seung-Hui Cho

Seung-Hui Cho, responsible for the Virginia Tech shooting in 2007, which resulted in 32 deaths, had a history of mental health issues. This case brought attention to campus mental health and the need for early intervention.

Cho had been diagnosed with severe anxiety disorder and had a history of depressive episodes and suicidal ideation.

The tragedy led to reforms in campus mental health services and protocols for addressing potential threats, as well as a discussion about gun laws and mental health.

The Aurora Theater Shooting and James Holmes

James Holmes, responsible for the 2012 Aurora theater shooting, was another instance where mental illness was a significant factor. Holmes was diagnosed with schizophrenia, and his mental state was a central aspect of the trial.

Holmes' defense centered around his schizophrenia diagnosis, arguing that he was in the throes of a psychotic episode during the shooting.

Holmes was found guilty and sentenced to life imprisonment. The case highlighted the challenges of addressing severe mental illness within the criminal justice system.

Chapter Nine: Rehabilitation and Reintegration

Different Therapeutic Models

Psychological approaches to rehabilitation are diverse, each offering different strategies and frameworks for addressing criminal behavior. These therapeutic models focus not just on reducing criminality but also on improving overall psychological well-being, which is often a key factor in preventing re-offense.

Cognitive-Behavioral Therapy (CBT)

- **Principles**: CBT is based on the idea that cognitive processes influence behavior and that changing negative thought patterns can lead to changes in behavior. It is one of the most evidence-based approaches in the rehabilitation of offenders.

- **Application**: In a criminal justice context, CBT targets criminogenic needs such as impulsivity, aggression, substance abuse, and poor problem-solving skills. Programs often include anger management, social skills training, and relapse prevention strategies.

- **Effectiveness**: CBT has been shown to be effective in reducing recidivism, particularly when tailored to the individual's specific needs and risk factors.

Dialectical Behavior Therapy (DBT)

- **Principles**: DBT is a form of CBT that focuses on teaching skills to manage emotions, tolerate distress, improve relationships, and live mindfully.

- **Application**: DBT is particularly effective for individuals with borderline personality disorder, a condition that is over-represented in criminal populations. It is also useful for offenders with emotional regulation difficulties.

- **Effectiveness**: DBT has been shown to reduce self-harm and suicidal behavior and is increasingly being recognized for its potential in reducing criminal behavior.

Psychodynamic Therapy

- **Principles**: This therapy focuses on uncovering and understanding unconscious thoughts and past experiences that influence current behavior.

- **Application**: Psychodynamic therapy in a criminal context might explore early life experiences, unresolved conflicts, and dysfunctional family dynamics that contribute to criminal behavior.

- **Effectiveness**: While more research is needed, psychodynamic therapy can be beneficial, particularly for offenders with complex emotional needs or traumatic histories.

Motivational Interviewing (MI)

- **Principles**: MI is a client-centered approach that aims to enhance an individual's motivation to change. It involves exploring and resolving ambivalence about behavioral change.

- **Application**: In criminal rehabilitation, MI is used to motivate offenders to engage in treatment and take responsibility for their change process. It is often used in substance abuse treatment.

- **Effectiveness**: MI has been found effective in treating substance abuse and can be a valuable component of a comprehensive rehabilitation program.

Group Therapy and Therapeutic Communities

- **Principles**: Group therapy provides a supportive environment where individuals can learn from others' experiences. Therapeutic communities are structured programs where group living and shared responsibilities are used as part of therapy.

- **Application**: These approaches are used in prison and community settings to address issues like substance abuse, aggression, and social skills deficits.

- **Effectiveness**: Group therapy and therapeutic communities can foster social support, accountability, and the development of pro-social behaviors.

Restorative Justice Programs

- **Principles**: Restorative justice focuses on repairing the harm caused by criminal behavior. It involves reconciliation processes between offenders and victims.

- **Application**: This approach includes victim-offender mediation, community service, and restitution programs.

- **Effectiveness**: Restorative justice programs can reduce recidivism and are particularly effective in promoting victim satisfaction and offender empathy.

Incarceration: Effects of Prison on the Criminal Psyche

Incarceration, as a response to criminal behavior, has deep and multifaceted effects on the psyche of individuals subjected to it. While the primary purpose of incarceration is to punish and deter criminal activity, its psychological impact can have a profound effect on the prisoner's psyche.

Psychological Impact of Incarceration

- **Loss of Autonomy and Control**: One of the most immediate effects of incarceration is the loss of personal freedom and autonomy. Inmates are subject to strict routines and rules, with limited decision-making power. This loss can lead to feelings of helplessness and dependency, undermining self-efficacy and personal agency.

- **Social Isolation and Detachment**: Prison often entails separation from family, friends, and community. This isolation can strain relationships and lead to a sense of social detachment. For many inmates, the lack of supportive social networks exacerbates feelings of loneliness and alienation.

- **Exposure to a Criminal Subculture**: Imprisonment can expose individuals to a criminal subculture. This environment may reinforce criminal identities and behaviors, particularly in overcrowded facilities where gang affiliations and a culture of violence are prevalent.

- **Mental Health Deterioration**: Incarceration can exacerbate existing mental health conditions or contribute to the development of new ones. Common issues include depression, anxiety, and post-traumatic stress disorder (PTSD). The stress of confinement, fear of victimization, and lack of adequate mental health services in prisons compound these problems.

- **Institutionalization**: Long-term incarceration can lead to institutionalization, where inmates become accustomed to the structure and security of prison life. This dependence can make adjusting to life outside prison challenging, often leading to difficulties in coping with freedom and responsibility post-release.

- **Behavioral Effects**: Prison life can lead to the development of maladaptive behaviors as coping mechanisms. These may include aggression, hyper-vigilance, or emotional numbing. Inmates might also adopt a façade of toughness as a survival strategy, which can hinder emotional expression and genuine social interaction.

Impact on Rehabilitation and Reintegration

- **Challenges in Rehabilitation**: The prison environment can be counterproductive to rehabilitation goals. The lack of rehabilitative programs, educational opportunities, and vocational training limits the development of skills necessary for successful reintegration.

- **Stigmatization and Reintegration Hurdles**: Ex-offenders often face stigma and discrimination post-release. This societal reaction can hinder their efforts to find employment, housing, and re-establish social connections, increasing the risk of recidivism.

- **Inadequate Preparation for Release**: Many inmates receive limited support in preparing for release. Without transitional services, guidance, and support, adjusting to life after prison can be overwhelming, leading to a sense of disorientation and a high risk of re-offending.

The Need for Reform

- **Reform of Correctional Facilities**: There is a growing recognition of the need for prison reform to prioritize rehabilitation over mere punishment. This includes improving living conditions, providing access to mental health care, and implementing programs focused on skill development, education, and therapy.

- **Post-release Support Programs**: Effective reintegration requires comprehensive post-release support. This includes housing assistance, job training programs, mental health services, and community-based support networks.

- **Restorative Justice Approaches**: Incorporating restorative justice principles in correctional systems can help address the harms caused by crime, promote healing for both victims and offenders, and reduce the psychological impact of incarceration.

Recidivism

Recidivism, or the tendency of a convicted criminal to re-offend, is a critical concern in justice system. Factors contributing to recidivism encompass individual, social and systemic elements.

1. Individual Psychological Factors

- **Untreated Mental Health Issues**: Mental disorders, when left untreated, can increase the risk of re-offending. Conditions like schizophrenia, bipolar disorder, and personality disorders require ongoing treatment and management.

- **Substance Abuse**: Addiction to drugs or alcohol is a significant risk factor for recidivism. Substance abuse not only impairs judgment but can also lead individuals to commit crimes to support their addiction.

- **Cognitive Deficits and Impulsivity**: Cognitive impairments and a tendency towards impulsive behavior can hinder an individual's ability to adhere to the law and make prosocial choices.

- **Lack of Remorse or Empathy**: Individuals who show little remorse for their actions or lack empathy towards their victims are more likely to re-offend.

2. Social and Environmental Factors

- **Peer Influences**: Associating with other criminals or being part of a criminal subculture can reinforce criminal behavior and increase the likelihood of re-offending.

- **Family Dynamics**: Dysfunctional family relationships and lack of familial support can contribute to recidivism. Family conflict, abuse, or neglect during childhood are also risk factors.

- **Socioeconomic Status**: Poverty, unemployment, and lack of education are significant contributors to recidivism. These factors can limit access to lawful opportunities and resources for rehabilitation.

3. Institutional Factors

- **Prison Environment**: The experience within prison can impact the likelihood of re-offending. Exposure to hardened criminals, gang culture within prisons, or lack of rehabilitative programs can exacerbate criminal tendencies.

- **Inadequate Rehabilitation Programs**: Rehabilitation programs that are not evidence-based, lack individual tailoring, or are insufficient in addressing the complex needs of offenders can fail to reduce recidivism.

4. Community Reintegration Challenges

- **Stigma and Social Isolation**: Ex-offenders often face stigma and social isolation upon release, making reintegration into society challenging. This social exclusion can push individuals back into criminal activities.

- **Lack of Support Services**: Insufficient access to support services like counseling, job training, and housing assistance can hinder successful reintegration.

- **Employment Challenges**: Difficulty in finding employment due to a criminal record is a significant barrier. Unemployment or underemployment can lead to financial strain and increase the risk of re-offending.

5. Systemic and Policy Issues

- **Criminal Justice Policies**: Harsh sentencing laws and policies that focus more on punishment than rehabilitation can contribute to recidivism. A lack of focus on restorative justice or individualized sentencing can exacerbate this issue.

- **Inadequate Post-release Support**: Lack of structured post-release support and monitoring can leave ex-offenders without necessary guidance and resources, increasing the likelihood of re-offending.

Alternatives to Incarceration

Community-based rehabilitation (CBR) offers an alternative approach to the traditional incarceration model, focusing on rehabilitating offenders within their communities rather than in prison settings. This approach is grounded in the belief that effective rehabilitation can often be better achieved in an environment that allows the individual to maintain social ties and receive support from the community. CBR encompasses a variety of programs and strategies aimed at reducing recidivism, addressing the root causes of criminal behavior, and facilitating the successful reintegration of offenders into society.

Philosophy and Principles of Community-Based Rehabilitation

CBR is based on several key principles:

- **Integration Over Isolation**: It emphasizes keeping offenders integrated with their communities, where they can maintain family relationships, employment, and social networks.

- **Personalized Support**: CBR provides personalized support to address specific needs of offenders, such as substance abuse treatment, mental health services, education, and vocational training.

- **Restorative Justice**: This approach often incorporates elements of restorative justice, which focuses on repairing the harm caused by criminal behavior and reconciling offenders with victims and the wider community.

- **Empowerment and Responsibility**: CBR aims to empower individuals to take responsibility for their actions and their rehabilitation process, promoting personal growth and behavioral change.

Types of Community-Based Rehabilitation

- **Probation and Parole**: These programs allow offenders to serve their sentences outside of prison under supervision, with conditions that may include regular meetings with a probation officer, drug testing, and participation in treatment programs.

- **Community Service**: Offenders may be required to perform community service, contributing to society in a constructive way while reflecting on their actions.

- **Electronic Monitoring**: This involves the use of electronic devices to monitor the offender's location, ensuring they adhere to the terms of their release, such as curfews or restrictions on entering certain areas.

- **Day Reporting Centers**: These facilities require offenders to check in daily and participate in various rehabilitative programs, including counseling, educational courses, and skills training.

- **Drug Courts and Treatment Programs**: Specialized courts for drug-related offenses focus on rehabilitation rather than punishment, often mandating participation in treatment programs as an alternative to incarceration.

- **Mental Health Courts**: Similar to drug courts, these courts deal with offenders who have mental health issues, offering treatment options and supervision in lieu of traditional sentencing.

Effectiveness of Community-Based Rehabilitation

- **Reducing Recidivism**: Studies have shown that CBR can be effective in reducing recidivism, particularly when programs are tailored to the individual's needs and risk factors.

- **Cost-Effectiveness**: CBR is often more cost-effective than incarceration, reducing the financial burden on the criminal justice system.

- **Social Benefits**: By keeping offenders within their communities and focusing on rehabilitation, CBR can aid in maintaining family structures and reducing the social stigma associated with imprisonment.

Challenges and Considerations

- **Community Safety**: Ensuring the safety of the community is paramount. Risk assessments are crucial in determining the suitability of an offender for CBR.

- **Resource Availability**: The effectiveness of CBR depends on the availability of resources, including skilled professionals, treatment programs, and monitoring technologies.

- **Public Perception**: Gaining public support for CBR can be challenging, especially for offenses perceived as severe. Educating the public about the benefits of rehabilitation over incarceration is key.

- **Integration with Law Enforcement**: Effective CBR requires close coordination between various entities, including law enforcement, social services, mental health providers, and the judiciary.

Success Stories and Failures

Through examining both success stories and failures, we gain valuable insights into what constitutes effective rehabilitation and where improvements are needed.

Success Stories in Rehabilitation

The Norwegian Correctional Service (Kriminalomsorgen): Norway's correctional system emphasizes respect, dignity, and rehabilitation over punishment. The model is based on the principle of 'normality', where life inside prison should resemble life outside as much as possible to prepare inmates for re-entry into society.

Inmates have access to educational programs, vocational training, and skill-building workshops. Facilities like Halden Prison are designed to mimic the outside world, offering comfortable living conditions, opportunities for employment, and recreational activities.

Norway boasts one of the lowest recidivism rates in the world, around 20%, compared to higher rates in more punitive systems. This success is attributed to the humane treatment of inmates, focus on rehabilitation, and comprehensive post-release support.

The Norwegian model demonstrates that treating inmates with respect and providing them with the tools and skills needed for life after prison can significantly reduce re-offending.

The Delancey Street Foundation (USA): The Delancey Street Foundation, located in San Francisco, operates as a residential self-help organization for substance abusers and ex-convicts. It functions on the principles of mutual restitution, self-help, and peer support.

Residents receive no formal professional counseling; instead, they learn through a variety of entrepreneurial enterprises run by the residents themselves, such as moving companies, cafes, and bookstores. The program emphasizes accountability, education, and vocational training.

The program has successfully rehabilitated thousands of individuals over its four-decade history. It reports that a majority of its graduates go on to lead successful, crime-free lives, with many gaining employment or pursuing higher education.

Delancey Street's success illustrates the power of peer support, the value of practical skills and work experience, and the importance of personal responsibility in rehabilitation.

Failures in Rehabilitation Programs

Boot Camp Prisons (USA): Model and Approach: Boot camp prisons, designed to resemble military training camps, were introduced as a way to instill discipline in young offenders. The regimen included rigorous physical exercise, strict discipline, and a structured daily routine.

Shortcomings and Criticisms: While initially popular, studies revealed that these programs had little to no effect on recidivism rates. Critics argue that the harsh discipline and lack of therapeutic intervention did little to address the underlying causes of criminal behavior, such as substance abuse, mental health issues, or lack of education.

Many states in the U.S. have discontinued their boot camp programs due to their ineffectiveness in reducing re-offending and the potential for physical and emotional harm to participants.

The failure of boot camp prisons underscores the need for rehabilitation programs to address the root causes of criminal behavior rather than relying solely on discipline and physical rigor.

Scared Straight Programs: Scared Straight programs involve taking at-risk youth to prisons to interact with inmates who describe the harsh realities of life behind bars, aiming to deter them from criminal behavior.

Evaluations of these programs have shown them to be ineffective and, in some cases, counterproductive. Research indicates that exposure to prison environments and criminal lifestyles can actually increase the likelihood of offending among participants.

Many organizations, including the U.S. Department of Justice, have advised against the use of Scared Straight programs due to their lack of efficacy and potential harm.

Scared Straight programs illustrate that mere exposure to negative consequences is not sufficient to deter criminal behavior. Effective prevention requires positive role models, skill development, and addressing individual risk factors.

Chapter Ten: Forensic Psychology in the Courtroom

Forensic psychology is a specialized field where psychology intersects with the law. Forensic psychologists provide valuable insights into psychological aspects of legal cases, from the assessment of a defendant's mental state to advising on jury selection and case strategy.

As Expert Witnesses

1. **Assessment of Defendants**: One of the primary roles of forensic psychologists as expert witnesses is to assess defendants in criminal cases. They evaluate the defendant's mental state, particularly in cases where insanity or diminished capacity is claimed. This involves a thorough examination of the individual's mental health history, current mental state, and understanding of the crime. The psychologist may administer psychological tests, conduct interviews, and review medical records to ascertain the defendant's cognitive and emotional functioning.

- **Detailed Reports and Testimony**: The forensic psychologist prepares a detailed report on their findings and may be called to testify in court. Their testimony can include explanations of the defendant's mental condition, the impact of mental illness on their behavior, and whether they meet the legal criteria for insanity or diminished capacity.

- **Ethical Considerations**: The role of the expert witness requires adherence to strict ethical guidelines. Forensic psychologists must provide objective, unbiased information and avoid advocating for either side in a legal dispute.

2. **Evaluating Credibility of Witnesses**: Forensic psychologists also assess the credibility of witnesses. This can include evaluating a witness's ability to recall events accurately, determining if a child witness is competent to testify, or assessing whether a witness's testimony may be influenced by psychological factors like suggestibility or trauma.

As Legal Advisors

1. **Jury Selection**: Forensic psychologists often assist in the jury selection process. They analyze potential jurors' backgrounds, attitudes, and biases that might affect their decision-making. Using this information, they advise legal teams on jury selection strategies to ensure a fair and impartial jury.

- **Behavioral Profiling of Jurors**: This involves developing profiles of potential jurors based on demographic information, responses to voir dire questions, and non-verbal cues during jury selection. The goal is to identify individuals who may be favorable or unfavorable to a case based on their predispositions or life experiences.

2. **Case Strategy and Trial Consultation**: Forensic psychologists provide insights into human behavior that

can inform legal strategies. They may offer advice on how to present evidence in a way that is understandable and persuasive to a jury. They can also help attorneys understand the psychological dynamics of their case, such as the impact of a crime on a victim or the motivations behind a defendant's actions.

- **Assessing the Impact of Testimony**: Psychologists can advise on the potential impact of different types of testimony, such as the effect of emotional witness testimony on a jury. They may also help prepare witnesses for testimony, coaching them on how to effectively communicate their experiences.

3. **Child Custody and Family Law**: In family law cases, forensic psychologists evaluate the best interests of children in custody disputes. They assess each parent's ability to provide a stable and nurturing environment and may make recommendations regarding custody and visitation.

- **Evaluating Parent-Child Relationships**: This involves observing and assessing the interactions between parents and children, looking for signs of positive or negative relationships. They also assess factors like parental mental health, history of abuse or neglect, and the child's psychological needs.

Evaluating Competence to Stand Trial

In the legal system, determining a defendant's competence to stand trial is a critical process that intersects with the field of criminal psychology. This evaluation is pivotal in ensuring that the justice system operates fairly and ethically, respecting the rights of individuals who may not be fully capable of participating in their defense due to mental illness or cognitive impairments.

Understanding Competence to Stand Trial

- **Legal Foundation**: The concept of competence to stand trial is rooted in legal principles that uphold the right to a fair trial. A defendant must have the ability to understand the charges against them, the consequences of the proceedings, and be able to actively participate in their defense. The landmark case Dusky v. United States (1960) established the criteria for competence, emphasizing both factual and rational understanding of the legal process.

- **Importance in the Legal System**: Evaluating competence is crucial because trying an individual who lacks the necessary cognitive or mental capacity undermines the integrity of the legal process. It ensures that justice is not only done but is seen to be done.

The Role of Forensic Psychologists

- **Expert Evaluation**: Forensic psychologists are tasked with evaluating the mental state of the defendant to determine if they meet the criteria for competence. This involves a thorough assessment of their ability to comprehend legal proceedings and effectively participate in their defense.

- **Assessment Techniques**: The evaluation includes clinical interviews, psychological testing, and a review of the individual's psychiatric history. Psychologists may use specialized tools like the Competence Assessment for Standing Trial for Defendants with Mental Retardation (CAST*MR) or the MacArthur Competence Assessment Tool-Criminal Adjudication (MacCAT-CA) to aid in their assessment.

Process of Evaluating Competence

- **Clinical Interviews**: The psychologist conducts in-depth interviews to gauge the defendant's understanding of the legal process, including the roles of the judge, jury, prosecutor, and defense attorney. The defendant's ability to make informed decisions about their legal strategy, including plea bargains, is also assessed.

- **Cognitive and Psychological Assessment**: Standardized psychological tests are employed to assess cognitive functioning, memory, reasoning, and overall mental health. This helps identify any cognitive impairments or mental disorders that might impact the defendant's competence.

- **Observation and Interaction**: Psychologists observe the defendant's behavior, communication skills, and overall demeanor. They evaluate their ability to communicate logically, understand legal concepts, and engage meaningfully with legal counsel.

Report and Recommendations

- **Detailed Reporting**: Following the assessment, the forensic psychologist prepares a comprehensive report outlining their findings. This report includes an evaluation of the defendant's mental state, cognitive abilities, and understanding of the legal proceedings.

- **Expert Testimony**: Often, forensic psychologists are called to testify in court regarding their assessment. Their testimony can provide critical insights into the defendant's mental capacity and competence to stand trial.

Ethical and Legal Considerations

- **Objective and Unbiased Assessment**: Forensic psychologists must maintain objectivity, conducting evaluations without bias towards either the defense or prosecution.

- **Confidentiality and Consent**: Ethical guidelines dictate that defendants should be informed about the purpose of the evaluation and its potential implications. However, traditional therapist-client confidentiality does not fully apply in forensic assessments.

- **Impact of Findings**: The outcome of the competence evaluation can significantly affect the legal process. If a defendant is deemed incompetent, legal proceedings may be delayed or altered, and the individual might be required to undergo treatment to restore competence.

Psychology Behind Jury Decisions

Jury selection and the factors influencing jury decisions are integral to the legal process, blending the complexities of human psychology with the principles of justice. This area involves examining how jurors perceive evidence, the influence of individual biases, and group dynamics within the jury.

The Psychology of Jury Selection

1. **Voir Dire Process**: Jury selection begins with the voir dire, a process where potential jurors are questioned by attorneys and sometimes by the judge. The goal is to identify biases or preconceptions that might affect their judgment.

- **Assessing Attitudes and Biases**: Forensic psychologists often assist in formulating questions that help reveal jurors' attitudes on issues relevant to the case, such as their views on law enforcement, the legal system, or specific societal issues.

- **Demographic Factors**: While demographic factors like age, gender, and occupation don't uniformly predict a juror's stance, they can provide insights into potential perspectives or life experiences that may influence their decision-making.

2. **Juror Profiles**: Attorneys often create juror profiles to identify desirable or undesirable jurors based on case specifics. These profiles are informed by psychological research and expertise, although they are not foolproof predictors of juror behavior.

Factors Influencing Jury Decisions

1. **Evidence Interpretation**: Jurors' interpretation of evidence is influenced by their personal experiences,

cognitive biases, and the persuasiveness of the presentation. Complex or technical evidence might be challenging for jurors to understand, impacting their decision-making process.

2. **Persuasion Techniques**: The way lawyers frame and present arguments can significantly impact jurors. Techniques like storytelling, emotional appeals, and emphasizing certain evidence over others can shape jurors' perceptions of the case.

3. **Credibility Assessments**: Jurors assess the credibility of witnesses based on both verbal and non-verbal cues. Factors such as demeanor, consistency in testimony, and perceived honesty play a role in how jurors evaluate witness reliability.

Group Dynamics in Jury Decision Making

1. **Jury Deliberation**: Jury deliberation is where individual perceptions and biases collide with group dynamics. The process of reaching a consensus can be influenced by factors like groupthink, where the desire for harmony or conformity results in irrational or dysfunctional decision-making.

2. **Leadership and Influence**: Often, one or two jurors emerge as leaders. Their ability to persuade and influence the rest of the jury can significantly impact the final verdict.

3. **Minority Influence**: A single juror or a small group of jurors holding a different opinion can sway the entire

jury, especially if they present well-substantiated arguments.

Challenges in Jury Decision Making

1. **Implicit Biases**: Jurors, like all individuals, have implicit biases that can subconsciously influence their decisions. Efforts like juror education and awareness can help in mitigating these biases.

2. **External Influences**: External factors, such as media coverage of the case, public opinion, and cultural attitudes, can indirectly influence jurors' thinking and decisions.

3. **Emotional Impact**: Emotional responses to testimony, evidence, or the crime itself can overshadow objective evaluation, leading to decisions based more on emotion than fact.

Eyewitness Testimony

The accuracy of eyewitness accounts can be influenced by numerous psychological factors, making it a complex and sometimes controversial form of evidence in legal proceedings.

The Nature of Eyewitness Testimony

Eyewitness testimony involves an individual recounting their perception of a crime or event. It can be a powerful form of evidence, often swaying jury opinions and judicial outcomes. However, the human memory is not a flawless record of events but a reconstructive process susceptible to distortion and error.

Factors Affecting Eyewitness Reliability

- **Memory Encoding**: The initial observation of an event is subject to perceptual limitations. Factors like distance, lighting, and the witness's physical and emotional state can affect how a memory is encoded. High-stress situations, especially those involving violence or weapons, can impair a witness's ability to accurately recall details.

- **Memory Storage**: Over time, memories can become distorted. This distortion can be exacerbated by post-event information, such as discussions with other witnesses, media reports, or suggestive questioning. These influences can lead to a phenomenon known as 'memory contamination'.

- **Memory Retrieval**: Retrieving a memory is also prone to inaccuracies. The stress of a legal proceeding, the format of questioning, and the passage of time can all affect a witness's ability to accurately recall an event.

Misidentification and Suggestibility

- **Lineup Procedures**: Identification procedures, such as lineups or photo spreads, can significantly impact eyewitness accuracy. Suggestive lineup methods, where the suspect stands out or undue focus is placed on them, can lead to misidentification.

- **Suggestibility**: Some individuals are more suggestible than others, meaning they are more likely to incorporate misleading information into their memory.

Children, for instance, are particularly vulnerable to suggestibility, although adults are not immune.

Psychological Research on Eyewitness Testimony

- **The Role of Confidence**: Eyewitness confidence is often used as an indicator of accuracy. However, research shows that confidence and accuracy do not always correlate. A witness can be highly confident in their recollection and still be incorrect.

- **Cross-Race Identification**: Studies have demonstrated that people are better at recognizing faces of their own race compared to those of other races, a phenomenon known as the "cross-race effect". This can lead to higher rates of misidentification in cross-racial identifications.

- **The Influence of Questioning**: The wording of questions can shape a witness's testimony. Leading questions, or those that imply a certain answer, can alter a witness's recollection of events.

Legal Implications and Reforms

- **Jury Instruction**: Educating jurors about the potential fallibility of eyewitness testimony is crucial. Jurors should be informed about the factors that can affect memory accuracy.

- **Reforming Identification Procedures**: Implementing standardized, non-suggestive lineup procedures can help reduce the likelihood of misidentification. This includes ensuring lineup

members resemble the witness's description and
instructing the witness that the perpetrator may or may
not be present.

- **Expert Testimony**: Forensic psychologists often
  provide expert testimony on the reliability of eyewitness
  accounts, explaining to the court the psychological
  factors that can affect memory and perception.

Final chapter: New Challenges and Future Directions

Criminal psychology, a dynamic and evolving field, continually grapples with complex questions and challenges. Despite significant advancements, there are numerous areas where further research is critically needed to deepen our understanding of criminal behavior, improve legal processes, and enhance rehabilitation methods.

Understanding the Root Causes

- **Biological Underpinnings**: While strides have been made in understanding the biological aspects of criminal behavior, including genetic and neurological factors, much remains unknown. Research into how these biological components interact with environmental factors to influence criminality is needed. This includes studying brain development, neurochemical imbalances, and genetic predispositions.

- **Impact of Early Childhood Experiences**: The role of early childhood experiences, including trauma, neglect, and abuse, in shaping criminal behavior is a critical area of research. Understanding the long-term psychological effects of these experiences can inform prevention and intervention strategies.

Assessing and Improving Rehabilitation Techniques

- **Effectiveness of Rehabilitation Programs**: There is a need for systematic and longitudinal studies to assess the effectiveness of various rehabilitation programs, including cognitive-behavioral therapy, educational and vocational training, and substance abuse treatment, in reducing recidivism.

- **Tailoring Rehabilitation to Individual Needs**: Research into how rehabilitation programs can be better tailored to the specific needs of different offenders, including considerations of age, gender, cultural background, and type of crime, is essential.

Influence of Social and Cultural Factors

- **Role of Socioeconomic Factors**: The impact of socioeconomic factors, such as poverty, education, and social inequality, on criminal behavior, is a complex area requiring further exploration. Research into how these factors interplay to increase the risk of criminal behavior can inform broader social and economic policies.

- **Cultural and Community Influences**: There is a need to understand how cultural norms and community dynamics contribute to or deter criminal behavior. This includes studying the impact of community policing, neighborhood watch programs, and cultural attitudes towards crime and punishment.

Legal Process and Decision Making

- **Jury Decision Making**: Despite existing research, there is still much to learn about how juries make decisions, including the effects of individual biases, group dynamics, and the presentation of evidence. Understanding these factors can improve the fairness and effectiveness of trials.

- **Eyewitness Testimony**: Further research is needed to develop more reliable methods for assessing and enhancing the accuracy of eyewitness testimony, considering factors such as memory decay, stress, and suggestibility.

- **Insanity Defense**: The insanity defense remains a contentious and poorly understood area. More research into how mental illness impacts criminal responsibility and the effectiveness of legal standards in different jurisdictions is required.

Technological Advancements and Crime

- **Cybercrime**: As technology advances, so do the methods of committing crime. Research into the psychology of cybercriminals, the impact of technology on traditional forms of crime, and effective prevention and intervention strategies is urgently needed.

- **Digital Forensics**: The field of digital forensics is rapidly evolving. Research into how digital evidence can be effectively used in criminal investigations, while ensuring privacy and ethical considerations, is crucial.

Global Challenges

Criminal psychology, in a global context, confronts a diverse array of challenges that stem from differing legal systems, cultural norms, and societal structures. In an increasingly interconnected world, these challenges require a multifaceted and culturally sensitive approach.

Cultural and Legal Diversity

- **Varied Legal Frameworks**: Different countries operate under varied legal frameworks, ranging from common law systems to civil law and religious law systems. This diversity affects how crimes are defined, prosecuted, and punished. As a result, criminal psychologists must navigate these legal landscapes, understanding the implications for assessment, treatment, and rehabilitation of offenders.

- **Cultural Perceptions of Crime and Justice**: Cultural norms significantly influence perceptions of crime, justice, and rehabilitation. For instance, what constitutes a criminal act in one culture may be seen differently in another. The role of shame, honor, and communal versus individualistic perspectives on justice varies widely, affecting both the prevention of crime and the treatment of offenders.

Cross-Border Crimes and Cybercrime

- **Human Trafficking and Drug Trafficking**: These global issues require an understanding of the psychological mechanisms behind victimization and perpetration. This includes the impact of coercion, exploitation, and trauma on victims, and the motivations and organizational structures of criminal networks.

- **Cybercrime**: The rise of cybercrime presents unique challenges, as it transcends traditional geographic boundaries. Understanding the psychology of cybercriminals, who often operate in anonymity and may not see the immediate impact of their actions, is essential for developing effective prevention and intervention strategies.

Terrorism and Radicalization

- **Psychological Understanding of Terrorism**: The global threat of terrorism requires a deep understanding of the psychological factors that lead to radicalization. This includes studying the processes of indoctrination, the appeal of extremist ideologies, and the social and psychological profiles of terrorists.

- **Prevention and Deradicalization Programs**: Developing effective deradicalization programs and strategies to prevent the spread of extremist ideologies is a significant challenge. This requires collaborative international efforts and a nuanced understanding of the cultural and societal contexts in which radicalization occurs.

Migration and Cultural Integration

- **Impact of Migration**: Increasing global migration raises challenges regarding cultural integration, discrimination, and identity. Understanding the psychological impact of migration, acculturation stress, and the experience of refugees and asylum seekers is crucial for addressing related criminal justice issues.

- **Cultural Competence in Criminal Psychology**: There is a growing need for cultural competence in criminal psychology practices. Professionals must be equipped to work effectively with individuals from diverse cultural backgrounds, respecting different values, beliefs, and customs.

Human Rights and Ethical Considerations

- **Human Rights in Criminal Justice**: Ensuring that criminal psychology practices uphold international human rights standards is a global challenge. This includes addressing issues of torture, inhumane treatment in prisons, and fair trial rights.

- **Ethical Dilemmas**: Criminal psychologists face ethical dilemmas that can vary in different cultural and legal contexts. Balancing respect for cultural practices with ethical standards in psychology is a complex and ongoing challenge.

International Collaboration and Research

- **Sharing Knowledge and Best Practices**: There is a need for increased international collaboration in research and practice. Sharing knowledge, research findings, and best practices can aid in understanding the diverse manifestations of criminal behavior and effective interventions.

- **Global Research Initiatives**: Conducting cross-cultural research and developing globally relevant theories of criminal behavior are essential for the advancement of the field.

The Future of Criminal Psychology

The field of criminal psychology stands at the cusp of significant transformation, driven by technological advancements, evolving societal norms, and a deeper understanding of the human psyche. As we look towards the future, several key trends and predictions emerge, indicating the directions in which criminal psychology is likely to evolve. These developments promise to reshape our approaches to understanding, preventing, and responding to criminal behavior.

Technological Advancements and Their Impact

- **Digital and Cyber Psychology**: With the rise of digital technology and cybercrime, criminal psychologists will increasingly focus on understanding online behavior. This includes studying the psychological profiles of cybercriminals, the impact of digital footprints in profiling, and the psychological effects of cyberbullying and online radicalization.

- **Artificial Intelligence and Machine Learning**: AI and machine learning are expected to play a significant role in criminal psychology. These technologies can assist in analyzing vast amounts of data for pattern recognition, predicting criminal behavior, and identifying potential threats. However, they also raise ethical concerns regarding privacy and the potential for bias.

- **Virtual Reality (VR) in Rehabilitation**: VR technology may become a tool for rehabilitation, allowing offenders to experience empathy-inducing scenarios or practice social skills and decision-making in a controlled environment.

Integrating Neuroscience in Criminal Psychology

- **Neurobiological Research**: Advances in neuroscience will deepen our understanding of the biological underpinnings of criminal behavior. This includes exploring genetic factors, brain abnormalities, and neurochemical imbalances associated with aggression, impulsivity, and antisocial behavior.

- **Brain Imaging in Legal Contexts**: There is potential for increased use of brain imaging techniques in legal contexts, both in assessing the mental state of defendants and in lie detection. However, this also poses ethical and practical challenges regarding the interpretation and admissibility of neuroscientific evidence.

Social and Cultural Dynamics

- **Globalization and Cross-Cultural Studies**: As societies become more interconnected, there will be a greater need for cross-cultural research in criminal psychology. Understanding how cultural, social, and economic factors influence criminal behavior will be crucial for developing effective global strategies to combat crime.

- **Changing Crime Patterns**: Societal changes, such as shifts in drug use patterns, attitudes towards sexuality, and the impact of social media, will influence the nature of crimes committed. Criminal psychologists will need to adapt to these changing patterns in their research and practice.

Focus on Prevention and Early Intervention

- **Predictive Policing**: The future of criminal psychology will likely see an increased emphasis on predictive policing – using data analytics to prevent crimes before they happen. This will involve identifying risk factors and intervening early, particularly in youth populations.

- **Community-Based Approaches**: There will be a shift towards community-based strategies in both preventing and responding to crime. This includes community policing, rehabilitation programs that involve community support, and restorative justice practices.

Rehabilitation and Reintegration

- **Evidence-Based Rehabilitation**: The future will emphasize evidence-based rehabilitation methods. This includes tailored treatment programs that address individual risk factors and needs, with a focus on mental health treatment, education, and skill development.

- **Reintegration Support**: Enhanced support for the reintegration of ex-offenders into society will be a key trend. This involves not just correctional rehabilitation but also post-release support, including job training, housing assistance, and mental health care.

Educational Pathways: Preparing the Next Generation of Criminal Psychologists

As the demand for skilled criminal psychologists grows, educational pathways for aspiring professionals in this field are becoming increasingly important. These pathways not only provide the foundational knowledge and skills required but also prepare students to navigate the ethical and practical challenges they will encounter in their careers.

The journey to becoming a criminal psychologist typically begins with an undergraduate degree in psychology. This foundational stage offers a broad understanding of psychological principles, theories, and research methods. Core subjects often include developmental psychology, abnormal psychology, social psychology, and biopsychology. An understanding of basic psychological concepts is crucial as it lays the groundwork for more specialized knowledge in criminal psychology.

Following undergraduate studies, prospective criminal psychologists must engage in more focused and advanced training. This usually involves obtaining a graduate degree – either a master's or, more commonly, a doctoral degree. Specialized graduate programs in forensic psychology or criminology offer in-depth knowledge related to criminal behavior, legal processes, and the assessment and treatment of offenders. Coursework typically covers areas such as forensic assessment, psychopathology, psychological profiling, and the treatment of criminal populations. These programs also emphasize research skills, as the ability to conduct and interpret research is essential for evidence-based practice.

Practical experience is a pivotal component of training in criminal psychology. Graduate programs often include internships or practicum placements in settings such as correctional facilities, law enforcement agencies, courts, or mental health centers. These experiences provide invaluable real-world insights and an opportunity to apply theoretical knowledge in practical contexts. They also offer a glimpse into the day-to-day responsibilities and challenges faced by criminal psychologists, ranging from conducting assessments and providing expert testimony to engaging in rehabilitation and treatment interventions.

Licensure is another critical step for those seeking to enter the field of criminal psychology. The requirements for licensure vary by region but typically include completing a certain number of supervised practice hours and passing a licensing examination. In some jurisdictions, additional certification in forensic psychology may be required or recommended. Licensure not only ensures that practitioners meet professional standards but also instills confidence in their competencies among clients, colleagues, and the legal system.

Continuing education is crucial in this ever-evolving field. Criminal psychologists must stay informed about the latest research findings, emerging trends, and best practices. This ongoing learning can take the form of attending workshops and conferences, engaging in professional development courses, and staying active in professional organizations. Participation in these activities facilitates professional growth and helps practitioners remain responsive to changes and advancements in the field.

Beyond formal education and training, certain personal attributes and skills are vital for success in criminal psychology. These include strong analytical and critical thinking skills, the ability to communicate effectively, both in writing and verbally, and a high level of emotional intelligence. Given the often sensitive nature of the work, criminal psychologists must also possess empathy, patience, and the ability to maintain professional boundaries.

As the landscape of crime and justice continues to evolve, driven by societal changes and technological advancements, the educational pathways for criminal psychologists must also adapt. Future curriculums might place a greater emphasis on topics such as cybercrime, international criminal law, and the use of technology in psychological assessments and interventions. There may also be a growing need for cross-cultural competence, given the increasingly global nature of crime and the diverse populations that criminal psychologists serve.

Afterword

Criminal psychology helps us understand the complex nature of criminal behavior. By delving into the psychological underpinnings of why individuals commit crimes, this field sheds light on the motivations and circumstances that lead to such actions. Criminal behavior should be seen not only as a violation of legal norms, but also as a symptom of underlying psychological, social, and environmental problems.

By identifying risk factors associated with criminal behavior, psychologists have contributed to the development of early intervention programs. These initiatives aim to prevent criminal behavior before it occurs, particularly among vulnerable populations such as at-risk youth. This proactive approach has the potential to not only reduce crime rates but also to alleviate the social and economic burden associated with criminal activities.

Criminal psychology sits at the intersection of human behavior, law, and social norms, offering the insights needed to advance justice and improve society.

I hope that this handbook has served as a beacon for those interested in the nature of criminal behavior and methods of effective counteraction. I believe that raising public awareness of criminal psychology is the way to bring about tangible changes in people's lives and the structure of society.